Life: *The ...* *Of Your Soul*

The Journey Back To Love

To Gemini,

May your "50 is the new 40" message circle the world so one day I can see you on big billboards changing the world how I see it! Wish you the courage to see it through!

Love,

Laura Hurubaru

CONTENT

Dedication _____v

Acknowledgements _____ vi

Author bio _____ viii

Praise for Life: The Furnace Of Your Soul _____ ix

Foreword_____ xiii

Prologue – When Life Happens To You_____ viv

CHAPTER 1: NUMB TO THE CORE_____1

CHAPTER 2: OPEN FOR BUSINESS _____7

CHAPTER 3: ARE YOU GAME? _____ 14

CHAPTER 4: HAVING IT ALL _____ 19

CHAPTER 5.0: CONNECTING THE DOTS _____24

CHAPTER 5.1: AWARENESS _____26

CHAPTER 5.2: ASKING AND RECEIVING HELP _____33

CHAPTER 5.3: COURAGE _____43

CHAPTER 5.4: FAITH_____53

CHAPTER 5.5: SURRENDER _____62

CHAPTER 5.6: INTEGRITY _____ 68

CHAPTER 5.7: COMMITMENT _____74

CHAPTER 5.8: ACKNOWLEDGE YOURSELF_____ 82

CHAPTER 5.9: FORGIVENESS_____ 90

CHAPTER 5.10: LOVE YOURSELF _____96

CHAPTER 5.11: TIME _____ 104

CHAPTER 5.12: BECOMING/ASCENDING _____ 114

CHAPTER 6: SAYING A YES TO YOURSELF _____119

CHAPTER 7: THE DIRECTION TO TAKE_____ 130

CHAPTER 8: THE JOURNEY TO LOVE _____ 132

END OF THE BOOK TOOLS AND NOTES _____ 136

CONNECT WITH ME _____ 161

Dedication

To my beautiful twins, Rebeca and Casian. You make me want to be a better person every day, because you deserve the best mum one can ever dream of having.

I love you to the moon and back and this book is for you to never forget this.

Acknowledgements

There have been a lot of people in my life that have contributed to me being where I am today. And plenty of others who will help me to reach the next level.

Some might have helped me without me even realising it, but to those who I know that without them I wouldn't be here, I want to use this occasion and share special thanks.

If it wasn't for these special people in my life, this book would not have been written. Not by me anyway.

To Gabi, my sweetheart, you've been there every step of the way on my healing journey of me coming back to myself. You have been the solid ground I was uprooted from, the safety I have always craved for, the love I couldn't offer myself. There aren't enough words in this world for me to be able to thank you enough for all the support you've offered me.

To Kent Madsen, the person who set me on the path of self - discovery and personal development. It was your acknowledgement, which came at a divine time that allowed me to open up and accept the help that I immensely needed, but I was too afraid to admit that I did. I wouldn't have written this book if I would have not chosen this path. You helped me make the choice.

To Samantha Houghton, who held my hand gently and firmly while writing it and helped my manuscript become a real book. I could never thank you enough.

To all of the coaches and healers who supported me, the list is too long to name absolutely you all. Each and every one of you have helped me take yet one more step forward. With all the tears, all of the fears and all the doubts. I hope you'll receive ten times more in kind.

And last but not least, I want to thank God; even though it felt like you left me, abandoned me and punished me, you've always been there for me, whispering softly in my ear: "tomorrow is another day, tomorrow everything will be alright, just be patient and you'll see. Have faith. I Love you!"

Author bio

Laura Hurubaru is the Founder of From Scratch to Cash FAST University.

After a long healing journey, she figured out her purpose in life and created her own process to help other women do the same. Through her unique system, she is helping thousands of women who've found success in the corporate world launch online profitable businesses built around their own purpose.

Laura herself remains remarkably humble, though she does acknowledge that the fearless fighter within her will always be there when needed.

"People say I'm determined and that I get what I want. I say that I live my life aligned with the beliefs and values I hold most dear. When faced with every hurdle in front of me, I find a way to clear the path."

You can read more about me here: www.laurahurubaru.com

Praise for Life: The Furnace Of Your Soul

Laura has an incredible way of reaching out to the reader and connecting on such a deep level that you truly feel acknowledged. Through courageously sharing her powerful story and incredible wisdom, she lovingly guides the reader on a journey of self-discovery. She leaves them with a certainty that there is a better way, one that will lead to the beautiful life they deserve.

- *Samantha Touchais - Business and Mindset coach*

I believe that anyone who has faced adversity in their life will be able to use this book, not only as a source of inspiration, but also to help them move through their own story and create a new, empowering one. Laura Hurubaru shares her story with vulnerability and with her words, is able to ignite hope and feelings of value for the reader. As a therapist, I would highly recommend this book to my clients who are struggling with creating a new story for themselves. And as a reader who loves self-development, I found the exercises in this book practical and helpful in realigning with what I know to be true but that is sometimes forgotten.

- *Iva Gojanovic - LICSW, Child and Family therapist/ Social and Emotional Skills Coach*

This book clearly stands out in the deep-diving oceans of self-help books for women! There are books that we know we want to read, that will cover everything we need and that we'll re-read them all over again to discover further hidden truths. This is without doubt, one of those books. This will serve a woman who wants to take inspired action, and more importantly, is offered a clear and simple map to finally retrieve buried treasure within. She will know where and how to start and where to go and where not to go. Being torn apart by my conflict of high aspirations, my true connection and the integrity that I stand for, I find that I am repeatedly drawn back to the dark clouds of my abusive past for ten long years. In this book I have at last found the true concept of self-love. Every struggling woman will indeed, instantly and deeply, connect to Laura's guidance. They will finally receive their long awaited birth of awareness to their inner strength recognition, self-appreciation and personal liberty.

- *Ermina Alagic - Holiday Home Academy Coach*

In her first personal development book, the author recounts the painful events that led to her leaving her family home at the age of sixteen, the impact on her wellbeing, and the decision to utilise the negative power of these experiences as ammunition towards transformation. Laura reflects on the influences that shaped her and points to the freedom arising from awareness, as well as the opportunity to realise her own worth and power. A range of exercises and tools will provide the reader with practical steps to embark on a journey of creating the life they want and deserve.

- *Ela Gohil*

I believe her. I've been at least half way of her journey and I can tell that she's telling the truth and telling it like it is. I saw myself in her self-development journey, although our life stories are very different. This book is primarily about love and hope, and only secondarily about hard work. Don't fall into the trap of hearing only the voice that tells you firmly "you have to do the work". Yes, you have to do the work, but you must love yourself and have hope. If you find yourself without any kind of hope right now, read this book and circle with a red pen all of the words and paragraphs that speak about hope – be it explicitly or implicitly. Don't focus on recipes, on solutions, on the process. Hunt for hope. At the end, you'll have a book full of red inked pages, you'll breathe hope and discover the "hard work" is actually "hard hope". And not only that, it makes sense to you. This is priceless and it will save lives.

- *Irina Nicoleta PhD*

This book is a total masterpiece as it is empowering, healing and entertaining. The purpose of this book is for the reader to discover their own healing and to achieve more for themselves beyond any dreams. After reading just three pages of this book, I already fell in love with it. I found this book very engaging with the power in helping abused people who do not feel good enough to gain the self-confidence to love oneself so they can accomplish more in life. I recommend this for anyone who wants to gain self-empowerment and establish legacy in either their personal life or profession for many future generations.

- *Anna Grotowska - Survival Coach*

This book is life-changing! You probably have heard at least a thousand times of how to change your life, which steps to take and how to do it, but still, you are here. In this inspiring book, you will find this collection of secrets on how to transform your life into one of success and enjoyment when you challenge yourself to step out of your comfort zone. Some challenges will be uncomfortable and scary, but if you trust in the process and are committed to it, you will transform yourself into the person you always wanted to become. Laura is your inspiration for how to change and transform your life even when it seems impossible. Like she said: 'We are all coal being pushed to go deeper to become a diamond'. If you want to change your life, open your mind and your heart, then take the first action of reading this book.

- *Urška Videmšek - Life coach*

Foreword

'Life: The Furnace Of Your Soul' is an inspirational, self-help book that captures the author's authenticity. Laura shares her heartfelt story of trauma and pain and how she has used her experience to support, help and guide others.

The book is empowering and reminds us of the importance of self-love and growth. Laura's great words of wisdom, 'Whatever happens in life, you will be okay, no matter what the circumstance', helps people understand the power of how the darkest times bring us to light and how the opinions of others should not impact who we are as a person.

Through Laura's honesty, this self-help book will guide others who are going through a difficult time and provides some excellent tools to heal and become the best version of yourself.

Thank you, Laura, for sharing your wisdom!

Foreword is written by Katie Scott
Author 'Taking worry of the classroom'
Owner of 'Little Sunshine Mindfulness and Yoga'
www.littlesunshineyoga.co.uk

Prologue – When Life Happens To You

Oh my God.

He's leaving me alone again.

Gabi is going to work and it will be about twelve hours before I see him again. Twelve hours of being on my own. How am I going to make it through today? It feels desperate, I am desperate.

Off he goes. As my partner stands in the doorway of our apartment, he slowly whispers to me. "Bye sweetheart. I love you."

"I love you too."

As I close the door behind him, the salty tears start rolling down my crumpled face. My body shrinks as though it's under a heavy weight. My heart feels like it is going to break into two and my chest will shatter under the pressure. And the thoughts start racing around in my head like my life is about to end, each one begging to be heard, vying for my attention.

God. What did I do wrong? How could I screw up so badly? This was supposed to be a happy moment so how can it feel so wrong? I used to be so strong and I fought everybody. But whom do I fight now? I can't fight me but I can't quit either! Oh, God, please help me.

I headed towards our bedroom and the ear piercing shrill sounds became deafening. In their matching cots lay my tiny innocent three-month-old twins, their faces turned a deep red and their eyes scrunched up as they exercised their lungs to full capacity.

Fuck. Shit. Nothing I do is good enough. I can't seem to even make my babies happy. I can't seem to figure this motherhood out because no matter what I do they always cry. They cry a lot. Oh God, I can't do this. Is this how my life is going to be now? I honestly don't know if I will survive. Why am I such a terrible mother? Please help me God.

As I was looking at them, not sure who was crying the most, I tried to figure out what was wrong this time. Waves of immense guilt for feeling this way suffocated me. I questioned why I felt so bad. Why couldn't I just be happy as other women can? Why are things always so hard?

I realised that my way of dealing with problems was no longer good enough. I can't quit on my children. I can't quit this situation.

I can't fight them. I can't fight God. I can't. The only person to fight is me and how can I fight myself?

And in that fraught moment, it became very clear that I had to make a decision. Do I go on about my life in the same way? Or do I change?

Will I find a better way or will I quit in the same way that I previously quit all my jobs because I was so unhappy?

In that moment I had to be brutally honest with myself as I realised - what choice do I truly have?

It's not like I could send my kids back to God.

And leaving them? What kind of a mum does that? I am sure there are plenty of mothers of twins out there on their own who figured it out!

And not forgetting, on top of that, I've made a promise to myself - **to never do to my children what my parents did to me!** I'd promised myself that if I brought children into this world that I would be there for them, no matter what. They will always know that they are loved and wanted.

I just couldn't break the promise. I had to make a choice.

Do I stay stuck, in never ending pain, blaming God for whatever is happening to me or do I choose to figure out a way to make it?

And I chose. I chose to find a better way.

Have you ever felt like this? Where no matter what you do, nothing seems to be good enough?

No matter how good your career is, something is not working in your relationship?

No matter how good your relationships are, you can't seem to be able to keep a job?

And no matter how good one area of your life is, you're struggling with the rest in some form or shape. It's exhausting to feel like you are constantly fighting and still not getting what you want.

Have you ever felt like that? Be honest.

If you can relate to my despair, because that's absolutely what it was, you've picked up the right book to help with that. I'm going to be very candid with you and I won't be holding back from telling you how it was.

There is a reason for why you're reading this right now and that may become clearer for you as we continue, but let it be known that you're ready! You're ready to find some peace. You're ready to embrace the hope that no matter how bad your past might have been, your future looks brighter.

I used to be like this for almost my entire life. It was one long arduous struggle and I battled everything that came my way. I don't think that I knew how to be happy. Having my twins at the age of thirty-two was the final straw that forced me to take a hard look at what I was doing and how, and to start taking responsibility for the results I was creating. Because I was creating them, and that can be the hardest pill to swallow.

And if it wasn't for my twins, I can promise you that I would have never have reached the place I am now. I would never have been able to achieve the level of success that I have managed to achieve so far. I would never have been able to become the mother that I am today. I would never have been able to become the wife, nor the business owner or the woman that I am today.

This book right here wouldn't have been possible if it wasn't for them.

Growing up within a dysfunctional family, with an abusive and angry father and a mother who emotionally blackmailed me in every situation for her needs to be met makes you a certain way. Experiencing emotional, verbal and physical abuse for sixteen years, I learnt that I was on my own.

And if I wanted something in life I needed to fight for it!

Does this ring any bells?

I thought things weren't meant for me, they just didn't seem to happen or feel possible for me. Somehow I always ended up in tears for one reason or another. Hard didn't cut it.

Stick with me until the final chapter and you will see not only that you can heal from whatever trauma or past wound you have, but you will also understand that the past has no bearing on the future. You will receive the guidance on what you need to do in order for you to remove conflict from your life. And if you really want to feel at peace, and know that life is happening for you and not to you, implement what you read in this book and your life will never be the same again!

Every step of the way, whatever you envision, no matter where you're coming from, you can achieve it.

And then for you to believe that you can have it all! And then some!

Because you can.

I promise you.

CHAPTER 1

NUMB TO THE CORE

I know that you don't know me right now and that you have no reason to believe me, but if you feel like your chest is contracting every time you pause to think about your life, and no matter what you do, the knot in the pit of your stomach is always there the minute you wake up, then keep reading!

Before I had my children I would wake up feeling numb. There would be a fleeting moment after the alarm went off when I was at peace, but it would vanish faster than the hot breath that evaporates on a cold window pane. Then the drag of getting myself out of bed made me hit the snooze button on that alarm obsessively, knowing I would get the same feeling again the next time it went off.

And I would keep doing it, sometimes for a full hour until the feeling would become unbearable and I would have to find something to focus on to make it go away. And by the time my eyes were open, my brain had become overwhelmed all over again as if it were all new, fresh and raw to start another day with. I wished I could linger in that blissful ignorance of waking up longer or not having to wake up at all.

"Shit, you won't go to the gym today either!" That would do it! The piercing sound of the inner critic's voice in my head weirdly helped to get me out of the paralysed state.

"You screwed up again. You can't seem to do anything right."

Then I had to summon up all of my resources to fight it. But at least I was not lying there in bed all day long like a dead person.

As I robotically got ready for work, I would visualise the shit I would have to face at work that day. Meeting my boss and having to put up with the lack of support, of understanding and recognition for everything that I am and do for the good of the company.

"The patronising, superior looking, I-know-it-all kind of guy, asshole."

"They are all a bunch of assholes".

"They have no clue on how to lead and they're telling me how to do my job!"

"Don't mind them! Go do your thing!"

Pushing the horrible thoughts aside, I would focus on the things I loved and enjoyed about my job. My world was IT and so I loved solving problems and coming up with new solutions quicker than anyone else. I loved being surrounded by smart people. And leading them and building the best teams. I felt vindicated every time a person in my team would come and ask for help and thanked me every time I did. Their loyalty was so humbling. There was nothing I would ask of them they would not do.

"If I could do just this all day... but instead I have to tiptoe around other people's egos. Fight my way through emails and spend my whole energy drained on stupid office politics bullshit!"

As the work day would come to an end, I'd be looking at the clock, with mixed feelings about wanting to go home soon. "Fuck, another day has passed and nothing has changed. Tomorrow I will have to start all over again. This rat race is killing me. I am sure I am meant for something more than selling my soul to people who can't even see and acknowledge the value I am bringing to the team!"

On leaving work, I'd call my partner, Gabi, and arrange to meet halfway on our way home. The conversation often went something like this:

"How was your day, honey?"

"You know, the same bullshit. I wanted to try something new today again, and they came up with yet another bullshit excuse about the right process" I'd say sighing heavily.

"Yours?"

"Ok-ish!"

Most of our evenings we'd go out to a mall where we could have dinner and then enjoy a movie. I did not want us to become couch potatoes so I refused to buy a TV. That forced us to at least get out of the house.

We'd get home and then go straight to bed. As my head hit the pillow I would put myself to sleep in silent tears, worrying what the next day would bring and wondering when I would actually feel like I was living.

And that was my hell. Pretty much every day. To top it off, the weekends were no different. Just more boring housework to get done. Watching how my life got sucked away with every sock I would pair, gasping for air every time I caught sight of the shopping list. Wishing I was somewhere else, doing something else. What? Well, I wasn't clear on that. But definitely not this!

"This isn't living. This is slowly and surely dying", I would think to myself.

And this thought would kill me even more as I didn't know if there was a way out! And if I would be able to find it!

But I knew instinctively that this wasn't the life that I wanted for myself.

And I kept thinking "how are all these people who go to work from 9-5 every day, able to bear it? I mean how do they do it?"

I didn't seem to be able to be happy even though I had a lot of things that many people didn't; a very well paid job, an apartment in our name, a car, a loving partner. Was I ungrateful?

"What else do I want?"

Your days may look different or they might look very similar to mine. What is important though is how you feel inside about them.

How do you feel about yourself?

How do you feel about your life?

Do you feel incomplete?

Like something is missing from your life?

Like there's something else out there for you, but you just don't know what that is or how to get it?

CHAPTER 2

OPEN FOR BUSINESS

I grew up in Romania, and I left home when I was sixteen.

Before I left, I woke up each day facing overwhelming fear and pain. My father was an abusive alcoholic. Every day his drunken, aggressive behaviour terrorized me, my mother, and my brothers. I desperately tried to help my mother and brothers escape our daily nightmare, but I couldn't do anything to make things better. I felt helpless but I soon realised that I had to do something different. I knew I'd be no help to anyone if I stayed at home; I couldn't help my mother, brothers, or anyone else if I was dead. That's when I decided to finally leave.

It was a strategic move, motivated by my desire to help my mother and brothers. Free from my father, I was able to pursue every avenue to help them; I contacted the police, lawyers, and any authority I could. Eventually, I guided my mom through her divorce. She was so immobilized by the abuse that most people would say that it was I that divorced my father. The day we went to the divorce trial is a memory that is etched in my mind; my brothers hid behind me in fear and my mother self-medicated to stop the trembling that shook her body.

When I left home I convinced myself that if I worked hard I wouldn't need anyone; I could take care of myself. I was fiercely determined and set off to take control of my life.

I put myself through University. I committed and worked hard to earn scholarships so that the university could help with providing a roof over my head, food, tuition and books to study from. I lived with four other girls who were also students. I knew that if I made good grades I could take care of all of my needs and continue to help my family. I decided to study computer science because I was good at mathematics and I couldn't afford tutors, so I chose a major that I could mostly teach to myself.

After two years, the scholarship was no longer enough to cover the costs of the hostel, my groceries and inflated tuition. I had met my life partner, and we started a small printing business to keep us afloat until I had graduated in 2003. Together, we supported each other – I used to cook, and Gabi had a computer which I was able to use for my studies. While my partner and I lived in a tiny apartment, we waited for me to find my first job. When I landed my new role, we finally had enough money to pay for a house with the help of a small loan. Our brothers stayed with us often, and I was able to help put them through school also to create a better future for themselves. I knew more than anything that I was right, and I proved that if you studied hard then you can be independent and self-sufficient.

I was good and efficient at my job as a software developer. I could pinpoint exactly where the technical problems were and how to fix them. For a time I didn't worry too much about what I wanted in life because I was still in survival mode and was without the awareness. However, I became accustomed to this new world which was so far removed from my origins. I couldn't always explain the root of the problems we faced to my bosses, but my creative problem-solving and unique approach would always fix the issue.

What I didn't realise was that corporate success depends on social relationships and navigating the jungle of office politics. I kept climbing the company ladder, but I didn't feel appreciated for the work I did. I got results but I didn't understand or desire to play the social games. I tried asking for raises and bonuses, but because I was so attached to the result, I fell short. I was too emotional, and I didn't feel like I had the tools to handle the hardened political nature of the corporate world. The only way I would get what I wanted was when I quit my current job and found another, giving me what I wanted. I kept running into the same obstacles and it became a destructive cycle.

Struggling with this made me feel awful; I felt like I wasn't normal. I dug my heels in and refused to give up and I was determined to find a place that would value me and the results I brought to the workplace. I felt like I'd known how to manoeuvre my way through at school, but not in the corporate environment. Most managers had no clue how to manage someone like me and I realised that I was training my bosses on how to manage me.

Coding soon began to bore me. I was motivated to work with people and I found a position as a junior team leader where I found success. I was talented at putting teams together that worked like clockwork. I started to flourish and thought that my day had finally arrived. However, I ran into the same problem, I wasn't valued for what I brought to the business. Even though I was successful, my boss would not raise my salary. It was most frustrating and I had to find another job to pay me what I was worth. I kept doing that until eventually, I started getting fired, because now I had the proof that I knew how to get better results than my peers, and even my managers in leading my teams. It didn't go down well.

As the pattern continued, I was fired again from my next job. It was a shock to my system. I knew that I was different; I had a completely different approach to problem-solving and dealing with people. Although my way of working yielded results, I felt like a failure. I sought out an NLP coach and psychologist, who helped me to recover. That's when I realised the corporate world wasn't for me. I didn't want to climb the company ladder. I refused to spend fifteen years prematurely gaining white hair to finally do what I want. I wanted to be my own boss and I started freelancing, consulting and learning about leadership.

My maternal clock was ticking and I soon wanted to start a family. My partner and I struggled through seven years of trying to get pregnant before finally deciding to try IVF. We were still living in Romania, and although I wanted to have my own online business, it was unheard of there. No one understood what I was trying to do. The IVF treatments were extremely difficult and emotionally demanding, but in the end, we succeeded and I gave birth to our twins. The idea of an online business became even more attractive as it would mean that I could stay home with my babies and not deal with incompetent bosses.

While I was pregnant I studied Brendon Burchard's Expert Academy, Reiki, energy healing, personal development, and many other programs to help me succeed in the online world. However, after I gave birth I went through a period of bleak darkness. I was consumed with worry and anger. I was overwhelmed with being a new mom and frustrated that I didn't have time to even shower or sleep. I didn't know who I was, and every label I put on myself felt too limiting. I punished myself for not succeeding, even though my plate was full. I eventually went back to my NLP coach, but the **strategies weren't working** – I needed something else.

She referred me to a friend who introduced me to pranic healing and past-life regression healing. I soon recognised how I was hurting myself, my kids, my partner, and I experienced profound breakthroughs. It was magical.

Shortly after, we moved to London. I took one more job but promised myself it would be the last job I ever had. I was determined to make my dreams of having my own online business a reality.

I took Harv Ecker's Millionaire Mind course and attended Tony Robbins' UPW (Unleash the Power Within) mega event. And for the first time in my life, I was focused on honouring myself. I knew it was time to concentrate on my dreams of having my own business. I wanted to give value to people. Although I had grown a lot, I was still stalling on my success. I wasn't taking action on the things I needed to do to succeed. Deep down, I knew that if I failed this time it wouldn't be for the same reasons as in the past. I knew I had ideas; creative ideas that filled up my mind with possibilities. And it hit me – maybe someone out there would buy my ideas! I was stepping into my power and wielding it to make a difference in people's lives.

It was incredible seeing something that was envisioned in my mind, alive, and out in the world. That's when I knew I had a gift. I have so many ideas, and I could help people who struggled with ideas of their own. I could help them see the natural talents they have and to package it into a program. I knew I could do whatever I set my mind to. Enthusiastically, I soon created a second program and sold that as well. I knew I had something amazing that could really help people.

Everything connected together. I put my idea of how I helped people come up with lucrative programs aimed at coaches and healers on Facebook. Immediately I had women sign up. I was officially open for business!

CHAPTER 3

ARE YOU GAME?

I know what you must be thinking now. That somehow I must be special, or incredibly smart or lucky and that you don't have that! I know because I have had those exact same thoughts myself.

I remember watching Tony Robbins' videos on Youtube as he would coach other people and be amazed and moved to tears by the shifts I would see in people after he told them his truth. Why does it seem to work for him and when I do it nobody seems to notice or give me credit?

Or Richard Branson - I used to love and admire his free spirit and his "screw it let's do it" mantra. He seemed to make every idea he had into a multi-million dollar business and I wasn't even able to get started with one. Just one. And I was having millions of ideas!

Or what about Robin Sharma, teaching leadership after he changed his career from being a lawyer? I mean, he never led a team ... how can he talk about something like that and get paid for it?

And I kept asking myself what is that they've got that I don't?

Are they smarter than you? Is it something only 'the chosen' ones possess?

I mean you've probably tried everything under the sun and exhausted a lot of strategies, right?

You've read tonnes of personal development books on how to better yourself, how to master your emotions, heal past trauma, how to love yourself, spirituality titles and literature on how to find your purpose...

Maybe you've spent years sitting in a counsellor's room and while the sessions make you feel a bit better in the moment, when you're on your own at home again, that gnawing feeling in the pit of your stomach is back there again?

"This is never going to end... What if I will always feel this miserable?" - you might think to yourself.

You've tried coaching, and while setting goals such as having a better job with greater pay would be achieved, it really felt like you were just changing the decor. It was still you just moving from one room to the next: in one space there was ocean blue decor, in the next spring green walls and suchlike. But ultimately, in other respects, everything stays the same. And that feeling of "the same old same old" refuses to be shaken off.

I mean, what does one need to do to have it all? To feel complete and fulfilled?

One of my favourite quotes: **I am not who I am today because of my challenges. I am who I am today because of my choices!** (I came out with this one, after I got fed up with people telling me how my past and my abusive father helped me be the strong person I am today). If I hadn't made different choices I may still have been in a situation I didn't want to be in.

At every turn you're somewhere you've never been before. You finish at University, the next thing on your list would be to get a job. Having children would not even cross your mind. After a while you settle and create the family you wished you had when you were a child. Suddenly, what was of interest to you in your twenties no longer appeals to you.

In a similar way, if you read the same book in your twenties you will take different things out of it as if you would read it in your forties. Why? You are no longer the same person. Your choices created other choices and so on and so forth.

This is no different to the tools, techniques and methods you might have tried already to help your situation; the coaching, the counselling, the alternative therapy. They will all have different results if you apply it to a topic you've barely started scratching the surface of, as opposed to something you've continuously worked on.

Why? You understand more about the situation every time and you go deeper every time and gather more insight.

Think about it this way: a diamond is nothing but a coal under immense pressure.

Coal is formed from heat and pressure, just like diamonds are. However, diamonds require greater temperatures and far more direct pressure to form, which is a primary reason why the end result is so different. This extreme heat and pressure can only be found much further into the earth. Since coal is formed near the surface, the heat and pressure are far less severe. When you just begin to work on your challenges, you're just really a piece of coal being pushed to go deeper to become a diamond. The trouble is, when people feel they are getting worse they assume what they are doing isn't working and they give up in the middle of the process. They don't go deep into the earth to manage to complete the process.

Can you see how this works?

Let's suppose if you were wondering how another book will manage to create a different impact for you, just use this opportunity to go deeper. Remember you're still a piece of coal under pressure. And the deeper you go, the closer you get to becoming a diamond! Believe in you and in your process.

Read through each chapter and take action every time I invite you to dig deeper. Be patient and be persistent.

My goal with this book is to offer you a more empowering perspective to your situation that you can then use and take action by implementing the processes and tools that I will share with you. They are what helped me and I am confident that if you apply yourself to them rigorously, you will get one step closer to the diamond that we both know is somewhere inside of you.

Are you game?

CHAPTER 4

HAVING IT ALL

I magine having everything you ever wanted! What would a typical day in your life look like?

This is how radically different my day, in a nutshell, appears now...

The alarm goes off at 5 am during the weekdays. I literally jump out of bed, looking forward to my hot bath with essential oils. I smile without reason and go about my daily routine like a kid excitedly looking forward to playing on their tablet.

A lot has changed in the last few years that I can't even begin to compare. At occasional times in my business I had to deal with an unhappy client. This would normally have reduced me to spiral in panic and withdraw, leaving me feeling not only a failure, but the worst person on the planet.

But not these days. Now I know that I am strong enough to deal with whatever life throws at me. I don't worry, I just confidently know. I know how to create safety and love within myself and as such, no matter how unpleasant the experience, I still show up and glow. Dealing with life has become so easy that I can't even recognise myself. I've mastered myself and my thoughts to the extent that my children don't receive the force of my anger when things don't go my way.

I truly and deeply feel FREE.

You see, most of the time, we are not afraid of what might happen if we walk our own path.

Most of the time we are afraid of our OWN POWER. We fear we might not use it ethically, that we might need to sell our soul to use it. Or that it will be painfully rejected. By admitting that we have it, means we have to take the responsibility for all of the situations where we went through hell. And sometimes we are more loyal to our wounds and to our abused victim identity than to the new elevated version of ourselves that is craving to get out. We attach ourselves to our mind, to our thoughts and this results in that we can't see the beautiful beings that we are.

Let me ask you this:

What if everything you think you know about yourself isn't true?

What if I told you that there is no predefined destination?

What if I told you that there is no 'right way'?

What if I told you the only way is YOUR way?

And that if you allow yourself this, you can invent yourself and change it anytime you want to?

Will you take me up on exploring how this might look like for you?

Great! Pick up a piece of paper and a pen! Find a space where you can just be with yourself!

Answer these questions in as much vivid detail as you can. Like you would describe a movie on paper:

If you were to let your spirit soar - what would you create?

How would you experience yourself daily?

If you were to be a magical being - what would you be? (You can make up one of your own.)

If you were to possess a magic superpower what would that be?

What magic will you create in your life daily?

Let your imagination flow. You are the author of your book. You just need to become a blank canvas first.

And don't worry about not making sense. Right now just learn to trust the creative side of you. The 'how' will show up when you've made the decision to go for it. I shall expand more on this further on.

We are such amazing beautiful souls. We have so many passions and interests. They weren't given to you to waste. They were given so the world can experience you and your gifts in the unique combination of your expression.

When you let go of controlling how things should look, or what you should be doing, or how you should be feeling, and instead, allow them to happen, you will have unlocked an immense reservoir of energy.

With that energy you can create anything you desire. You will feel things finally fall into place. You will experience ease. Things that used to bother you no longer have an impact on you.

You will feel unstoppable!

Believe!!!

Ready?

CHAPTER 5

CONNECTING THE DOTS

"You can't connect the dots looking forward; you can only connect them looking backwards. So you have to trust that the dots will somehow connect in your future. You have to trust in something - your gut, destiny, life, karma, whatever."

Steve Jobs.

I've read hundreds of self-development books, invested my time, energy and money, over £200K, in coaches and healers over the years, in search of the next thing that will help me to progress. I didn't know anything about most of them, I just followed my gut instinct. And it always paid off.

Looking back now on my journey I can recognise the big shifts I needed to make in order to move forward. And I now know that each step is built on the previous one. Pretty much like with computer games - you can't unlock the next level unless you've completed the existing one.

I have listed them in order to give you a clear structure to follow, which will also allow you to see the road ahead.

Understanding that it is a process and that it takes time will give you the confidence and the knowing to stick with it. I am providing you with the light at the end of the tunnel.

CHAPTER 5.1

AWARENESS

'Unless you make the unconscious conscious, it will direct your life and you will call it fate!'
- Carl Jung

OMG... If I had received a penny every time people told me how I sabotaged myself and I didn't believe them, or for every time I thought to myself "you nailed it/fixed it/got it" only to realise that I didn't... I would be a lot richer right now!

I was this strong person, who at 16 years old, left home and took life into her own hands.

"Who are you to tell me what I should do? You don't know anything."

I almost feel sorry for all the people who tried along the years to guide me and steer me on the 'right' path as I now know how big a task they had taken on!

At that time I thought they were all a bunch of assholes who were not seeing the 'brilliance' in me and were being intimidated by my being 'better than them'.

How silly - I can see that now!

And to make it more hilarious, I was going round in circles asking: "what am I doing wrong? Why is no one telling me? I'd like to change and to do something different. But I don't know what that is."

Until one day, a man, who I won't be able to thank enough in this lifetime, took me aside and said this to me: "Laura, you have the potential to do my job. But you can't go about solving problems by smashing through the walls every time things don't go your way. People can't see the light you see. You need to take them on a journey - not lash out.

I can help - if you want?"

I looked at this man with white hair and deep blue eyes. He was three layers above me in the management structure and was the right-hand man to the company CEO. I will never ever forget that moment. This man was telling me what I always knew inside. And he was not just any man - but a person who I dreamed one day that I would become. I wanted to have his level of influence and impact in a company, and ultimately in the world.

And here he was, not only recognising my talents but also offering to help! ME?

Somehow this generous offer melted some of the rigid defences I had built as a teenager to protect myself. All those aggressive times that I spent fighting my father who wished for me to end up as a prostitute, giving head in the street as a career! They were his words and you do not forget a phrase such as this.

This man's kind wisdom allowed me to reach the realisation of "There must be something you're doing Laura that you end up in the same situation over and over again. Maybe it's time to see that psychologist you always knew one day you would have to go to."

You see I grew up in an emotionally and physically abusive environment and I would fear for my life most of the time. I instinctively knew that this environment might have screwed up my head, and that I would need some professional help to help heal that. But it never felt like the right time. And money was always an issue. I felt that it was going to be expensive for something I wasn't sure anyone could help to fix. Would I be broken goods for the rest of my life? The fear of finally finding out I 'can't be saved' and 'helped', left me stuck without taking any real action to resolve it, continuing the same stubborn patterns.

Until K. He helped me to break the cycle. He instilled hope that it was possible for me to get what I wanted as long as I worked on myself and focussed on why I behaved the way I did. And this is how my journey with personal development started. And I've realised that without the AWARENESS of what I was doing, I wouldn't ever be able to change anything. I would keep repeating the same patterns. And I would always be unhappy and miserable even though it felt like I was 'trying' everything.

The truth is, we are all blind to what we are doing unless we train ourselves to become aware of our own thoughts and actions.

The easiest way is to have other people who are a few steps ahead of you that can help to mentor and coach you. They can see what you can't see yourself and help you shift those blind spots quickly.

Or at least spend time in networks that are filled with people who have already achieved what you are still trying to achieve.

And journal daily. Here are some questions you could ask yourself to help you be effective in your journaling and receive the awareness on why you feel the way you do, or behave the way that you do:

1. **What's upsetting me about this situation?**
2. **What pisses me off/angers/saddens me about this situation?**

3. **What do I think it will happen if...?**
4. **What's the worst that could happen if that was true?**
5. **What do I need to learn in order to deal with this effectively?**
6. **What am I refusing to see about myself in relationship with this situation?**
7. **What do I need to take responsibility for in creating this situation?**
8. **What are my next steps?**

The goal of journaling is to help you to slow down your thinking and put your thoughts on paper so you can analyse them. This isn't a process for you to start beating yourself up. It is a process to start recognising some of your thought patterns. When you start catching your thoughts you will be able to shift them, and choose them carefully so they are supporting you and not damaging you.

This is a never ending process. You will never reach the end of it. And I am not saying this to discourage you and keep you from even trying.

It's actually to help you understand that this work is a must. In order to take control of your life, you have to take control of your mind. Your mind will always do its thing - thinking thoughts. You always need to be vigilant to these thoughts.

Journaling and spending time with people who are at a different level of consciousness is the only way to grow awareness of your own level of awareness. They are the mirror that you need in order to grow.

Use it. And do it wisely.

I am personally always in a coaching relationship of some kind: either on a one-on-one basis or group coaching. And I journal daily, multiple times a day. It's a non-negotiable for me. That's how committed I am to this work. And that's how important I believe it is.

And even me, who I believe to be a bit of a masochist when it comes to challenging myself to grow and working on the stuff that I feel is keeping me back ... gets surprised absolutely every time by how little I still know.

Even with this example right here. I thought I'd got it when K came to me and shared it with me. But then, ten years later there was an incident that allowed me to see this pattern for what it was: a defence mechanism of not trusting, that was keeping me a prisoner really. And every time I would go out in the world, I would treat people with the same mistrust. Even if I was more inclined to listen to others, and I was aware now that I must be doing something wrong ... I still could not see it. I could not see how it was actually embedded in absolutely everything.

The worst of it all ... it was causing me so much pain and I could not see it. I was pretty much like a frog in boiling water. It was killing me softly and I did not see it for most of my life.

And it will be the same for you with some of the patterns you've developed over the years. Don't think you've figured it out just the once and then it's out of the door. It's not. I couldn't see it ten years back. And that was alright. The pain that came from awakening to the truth would have been unbearable for me to deal with at that time.

But ten years later, even if it hurt like hell, I was able to grow past it and let it go completely. I already had the tools to manage my state and my mind. Even so, it wasn't easy. It affected me for months.

You will learn the truth in stages at the times where you can handle it in the best way for you. But follow it no matter where it leads you, all the time. It will not lead you astray.

CHAPTER 5.2

ASKING AND RECEIVING HELP

"When you change the way you look at things, the things you look at begin to change"

~ *Wayne Dyer*

It takes practice and discipline to start being aware of your thoughts and the reasons behind why you do the stuff you do. And the commitment to keep doing the practice.

It takes courage to admit that whatever you experience is of your own doing, your own creation. And even more strength to admit that you need help and then accept it when it arrives.

Every person who went through any kind of hardship developed a hard-wired coping mechanism that instructed them to be self-reliant, and that they can't depend on anyone to come and save them. While this might get you through the crisis, the trouble is, is that it will keep you in one form of crisis or another. It becomes like an addiction as it thrives in crisis mode.

Therefore if you feel like you're always in some kind of conflict, whether at work, with your partner, with your parents, with your friends, and as though you can't be happy and satisfied in all areas of your life, it is because you're operating from a false sense of security, as every time you overcome the challenges you feel powerful and strong.

But it's just a chemical you've got addicted to. To the extent whereby you will create conflict just to experience that feeling of strength. How crazy is this? But you can see how it serves a need and loops you in.

It's pretty crazy I am telling you. When I got this realisation it really hit me hard like a firm slap in the face. I will probably never forget it. It happened while I was crossing the street going to work one morning. The thought just appeared loud and clear: "you're doing this to yourself".

I felt like I was running out of air and that I would crumble right there in the middle of the street. I don't know how I got through my day ... but I didn't die.

That thought really stuck with me and it helped me be more determined in seeking and getting the help that I needed. I didn't know then, not even one percent of the insight. But if I hadn't woken up to that hard truth I wouldn't be here where I am now.

And I really was ready for help. I didn't care what I had to do. I just knew that if it was left to just me, by myself, it would have taken me ages, or probably I'd never have been able to get out of the pain that kept me captive.

For the first time in my life, that I could remember, I let go of my pride and of me being able to do it all on my own, demonstrating how smart I was that I could figure things out. I decided that needing and accepting help doesn't take away all of that. It actually made me even smarter. I could get to my desired destination a lot quicker and a HUGE lot easier!

The way to test you are truly ready to receive the help that you need, is to think about the thing that you believe you absolutely can't do, but you would be required to do it for what you want to achieve. For example, if you imagine it will cost you all of your savings and you 'can't afford this' to happen, you are ready to receive and accept help when 'losing all of your savings won't be an issue anymore'.

If you're ready to say "even if this means that I won't, or that I have to - I am still doing this". Then you are ready! And I can guarantee you that the minute you make that decision in yourself, the help will show up almost instantaneously.

It happened to me so many times, that I no longer doubt our power anymore. It might not come in the form you expect. And this is where it gets tricky. You really have to start paying attention and take the action in the direction that is presented to yourself. As you are required to walk a new path, it will be something you've never done before, so don't expect to find something to confirm that you're on the right path. The signposts will really be different from the ones you've been used to previously. You will be required to take a leap of faith and trust the divine guidance.

"But what will this divine guidance look like?" you might ask. Very good question. I see so many women these days, especially in the spiritual community, who still confuse God and what's happening to them with their self-sabotaging patterns. In fact, I am pretty convinced that they are not even aware when and how they are actually sabotaging themselves. One thing I do know though, is that God will not have you killed in the process of sending you a message. That's more likely to be a part of you which is desperate to get your attention. God is much more subtle. It comes with a soft and gentle voice and message. You know the voice I am talking about - it's almost like a whisper, you wouldn't normally hear it. But when you go to sleep and everything quietens down, it comes back out of nowhere to be heard once more.

"But wait Laura! How do I know which voice is talking? I have so many in my head. How do I know it's God talking and not some part of myself? How do I know if what I am creating is a sign or actually a way to sabotage myself? How can I tell the difference?"

That my friend is the secret, the golden treasure we all chase through life. If we would all know it and if it would be so easy to hear it – then we would all be a lot happier and a more conscious race. But we're not.

To guide you, I give you two laws:

- Always assume that you're sabotaging yourself.
- Everything you experience is of your creation.

And let's now take it one by one: *always assume you're sabotaging yourself.*

One time I had a client, who went through so much (like most of my clients) and the fear of putting herself out there and taking steps in getting her business off the ground was so big that she created all kinds of accidents. And she was so convinced that God made it happen so she could stop and rest.

And secondly; *everything you experience is of your creation.* She one time almost broke her neck. And while my heart went out to her - she was doing it! God doesn't want you to die in receiving a message. God is not creating the pain. You are. And even if your inner critic says: 'how can I manifest a car accident when the other person hit me?' it's clearly a message. You can still take the responsibility that you did not hear the message the first time around, the second time, the third and so on and that it took you a car accident to wake you up!

Still, even in this case, I believe that the wise part in her had to stop her. And not God. God just makes sure that the situations and people in your life align with who you are at that time.

Do this to help you build your awareness and the ability to recognise it. This way, you won't have to go through dramatic events to start listening to it:

- **Think back to a time when you were nudged to change your life. Yet you chose to ignore it. And the feeling and the messages kept coming back over and over again, until something happened. See if you can pinpoint this moment!**

- **Now think of a time where you heard the voice telling you something and you did it right away; maybe it was to leave a relationship which wasn't serving you. Maybe to quit a job where you were not fulfilled. In this case the voice stopped.**

- **Can you look at these two instances and determine if it was the same voice? If it is then that's the voice you need to become more familiar with.**

- **Some things to help you along the way. Pay attention to where it is coming from; in your head or outside of you? From your left or right? From the front or the back of you? What tone of voice is it and how loud or soft is it? The more you pay attention to these elements the easier it will get to recognise it.**

- **And as a final check, when you tune into it and really listen, you will start noticing a sense of peace and calmness in your stomach. Because that's the voice of complete faith and trust. When you follow it you expand. When you go against it you contract.**

Everything you experience is of your creation. Our minds are brilliant. The reality you perceive is being constructed in every second with your thoughts and decisions. More and more science is proving this to be true. Quantum physics already proved that the wave changes based on who is observing it, and it also changes the locations it is being perceived from: i.e. "disappears" from point A if the observer believes it's looking at it in point B. Fascinating!

Your subconscious is truly manifesting all the programs /routines/beliefs/ thoughts that are being stored there.

The good part with this is that you truly can create the life that you want by sending the right commands. The not-so-good part is, it is so vast and it has many dark corners and there are layers and layers to it, that you can't possibly access it all and make it known to your conscious mind in a lifetime.

All you can do is train your conscious mind to catch the thoughts in the waking reality and then shift them with the ones that support what you truly want to create.

While the science is complicated, the truth is really simple. Your mind does it! And if you were wounded in the past your mind carries the wounds.

The best thing to do is to build on top of the tool I have shared with you in the previous chapter. And now look at the world around you and treat it as a mirror:

• **If you either admire or hate a person remember to think to yourself: I am THAT!**

• **And whether you like or dislike the situation you're in, ask yourself: what part of me created or aligned itself with this particular situation?**

When you think 'I am that' and you completely dislike the person:

• **What part of you allowed them to be in your life and what part of you gave them permission to behave the way they do?**

• **Where you might behave in a similar way?**

When you get this you will understand how powerful you truly are. This realisation is not meant to make you feel bad, although it will be painful to see how much suffering you're creating for yourself and that you're the one actually doing it.

In the beginning, you might need some external help to guide you with this. I use different divination card decks to help me intuitively grasp what is going on with and around me.

At each stage of my life another deck will present itself as an 'answer' to my prayers. I had one with Angels by Doreen Virtue, then Isis by Alana Fairchild and some others. At the time of writing this book I was using Animal Magic Cards by Alexis Cartwright.

Why you would want to use something like these is because their messages are always hopeful and full of positivity. And if you have a strong pattern of beating yourself up about everything ... you might not see things clearly by journaling because you will be attacking yourself then too. Having 'outside' help might get you to start telling yourself positive messages and when you journal, to actually do it in a way to be supportive and not damaging.

The reason I've shared the journaling tool is because some people rely only on the 'divine' to tell them what to do. But actually that 'divine' thing is another ego construct which is hard to spot. By taking responsibility for absolutely everything, you won't fall into the trap of thinking God is to be 'blamed' for everything, even if you might not do it consciously.

Try them both. And know that the more you take responsibility for your thoughts and actions, the more powerful you will become. The faster the changes will happen and the quicker the things you want will show up in your life.

This is a very fascinating subject and whole books have been written already on this. I hope you will take these simple tools and start using them right away.

Notice how it feels inside to know that you are truly in control: by controlling your mind!

CHAPTER 5.3

COURAGE

"It takes courage to grow up and become who you really are"

~ E.E. Cummings

Sometimes knowing what you're doing and why is not enough to change one's life.

For example, I knew that in order to free myself up from the pain of the past I needed to forgive my parents. I can't tell you how many times I came across this, how many times my brothers asked me to do it, how many people and coaches asked me to do it for myself.

And although "I knew" that is something that I MUST do ... I didn't do it. For more than thirty years I held tightly onto my need to be right about them. About what terrible parents they were. I didn't want to accept that they didn't know any better. I didn't care. The little angry child in me wanted revenge. I kept saying to myself: "Just because you have difficulties doesn't mean you should take them out on your children. What did the children do wrong for one to beat them up like animals? Nothing... there is

nothing a child could do to deserve the physical punishments."
And no matter how much people tried to warn me I was as
stubborn as hell. Nothing or no-one could budge me from that
viewpoint.

Until one day there were several situations that happened at
the same time and one of my clients really mirrored this for me. I
could see how unfair she was towards me and what she was doing
to herself, first and foremost. She would create all kinds of
accidents and incidents, some really life threatening, just to not
have to move forward with her life and her business. And she
would blame me and my program, claiming that it wasn't flowing
and that there was a reason why this or that happened to her. And
I agreed; there was a reason. Only her mind tricked her into
thinking that the Universe was doing that to her. I believed
differently; one part of her was that scared to expose herself that
she would rather die than to sit in front of people and tell them
what she was all about. Literally. And in tuning in to understand
more on how to support her, I realised how much pain she was
enduring and I could recognise myself a lot in her. She held a
mirror for me as well.

I don't believe in coincidences and as such I always ask
myself: How did I create this situation? Where am I behaving the
same as the other person does? What do I need to learn from this?

That's when things really clicked for me: I realised I was in constant pain ALL of the time and not only on these special occasions when something would happen at work or at the kids' school. ON those occasions the pain comes out as it accumulated and some of it needed to be released like a cooker under pressure. Sometimes you need to let some air out.

For the rest of the time, I thought that the pain I was feeling was normal and I would not sense it or see it for what it was. I just assumed it was normal for everyone. Constantly worrying, crying all the time when things didn't go my way, waking up anxious every day. That felt normal then. I couldn't even feel it. It's now that I get to actually see it for what it was and feel the actual pain I was in. At that time I was really numb which is sad, as you can't change something that you don't have awareness of.

I understood then that through the abuse I experienced, I'd become very tolerant to pain and I couldn't tell the difference. I didn't know what being without pain meant or looked like.

One image came to me so strongly that I will probably never forget it. It's not that I'd built walls around me to protect myself. I actually constructed an iron cage that tightly gripped around me slowly crushing my flesh and bones. The more stress I would experience, the less space there would be between me and the metal frame, until it reached the point where it would pierce my flesh and bones.

That's the structure I'd built around myself to not allow people to touch me. When I started seeing it for what it was, I decided to tear it apart. Even if that meant ripping my flesh and my bones off... I didn't care. I just wanted it off of me.

As I was carrying it with me everywhere I went, it regularly pushed people away. I would then ask myself what was wrong with me. I needed to free myself. I needed to let this pattern go. I needed to learn to TRUST. And becoming vulnerable again and understanding that that's what's going to happen next, takes great courage.

And that is something you will be required to do with absolutely everything you will have to work through. You will have to let some bits of you go and create something new in place of those old parts. The mind doesn't like uncertainty, the unknown. You will feel the FEAR in absolutely every bone of your being. And you will have to CHOOSE absolutely every time what's most scary: to live with the pain or with the unknown?

Because I made the decision to let that fierce protection go, the event that followed led me then back to my past and my wounds and the pain from those years resurfaced. This time instead of having the frame tighten around me, I decided to feel the pain. To be open and vulnerable ... and to finally let go of it completely.

As a result I was able to decide to write two letters: one to my father and another to my mother.

They were not forgiving letters. They were letters laden with all of the unsaid things from when I was a child. The harsh and unfair judgements, the bad language, the unexpressed feelings and emotions. I did not keep anything back. Even as I was writing them I could observe my resistance to say it like it was, feeling like I was too nice to them. And that part of me who always seeks validation from them that keeps interfering ...

But I did not let it. Not this time. I knew instinctively that unless I acknowledged the hurt, that unless I accepted I felt that way, I would never be able to move forward.

I burned the letters in a ritual of releasing all of the negativity associated with the content of those papers. I created a 'baptism' of born again space.

It takes courage to change what you know needs changing. Especially when you've been through traumatic events. You want to control the outcome. You'd do anything to avoid pain. Not knowing what is going to happen afterwards creates the same fear response like the trauma itself. To the brain, the chemicals released are the same. That's why it's so hard to see it by yourself, without outside help. Without realising, you're creating the same trauma response to you and your body: by trying to prevent what you're afraid of ... you're actually creating it.

A lot of people asked me throughout the years how I did it. How did I have the courage to stand up to my father? How did I have the courage to leave home at 16 years old? I struggled with the answer myself too. I thought it was because I was strong and that my mum was weak, so it was only natural. But it didn't feel right.

The more I went to events where a lot of people opened up about their abuse and traumas, and of how much they allowed it - to the point they'd attempted suicide ... the more intrigued I was. I wasn't perceiving them as weak characters, so how come I didn't take the drugs, abuse the alcohol, or attract the abusive partner? How come I stayed away from all of that?

One weekend the answer came, and it was so refreshing and so warming to my soul, that I knew that was the truth. It was also such a powerful source of relief as I always felt like I didn't have enough of it.

The key ingredient that will give you the courage to remove yourself from a toxic, difficult situation is the degree to which you love yourself! I realised that I had always loved myself enough to know that that wasn't love. That what my parents were doing to me was not normal and that I didn't do anything to deserve their treatment. I loved myself enough to know that I deserved more and better, and then I went after that.

That's what will help you CHOOSE between staying in a painful situation, or removing yourself from it, even if that means you don't know what's going to happen next.

Even if it took me a while, I kept browsing; no, this isn't it; not this one, still not it. Until l found it.

You see, you can't, you absolutely cannot allow your spirit to be desecrated if you have enough love for yourself. You just can't. It's the biggest sin!

But if you understand that you're precious and one in billions, and the chance for you to exist in this universe is so incredibly small (scientifically proven), you'll understand how truly singular you are.

You were not born on this planet to be the mockery of other people, to be the outlet of their anger and rage, even if these people were your parents, or to be someone's sex toy because of their insecurity and their need for an easy prey. It was never your role.

And I know it's hard for you to see yourself in any other way than those who hurt you so far assigned to you. Trust me that that's not how God sees you.

Ask yourself this: if you were truly divine light and your purpose is to shine as brightly as possible, how are you honouring the light that is you? How do you show yourself that you love and respect yourself? How do your actions reflect love?

Think of a person who you believe loves you unconditionally (if you can't think of one, think of God). What would they say to you now about this? How much would they agree with you? And if they were to guide you to gather more self-love, what would their advice be?

If you're having trouble with this let's do a visualisation exercise (read it first and then do it):

Take three deep breaths. And close your eyes. If it helps, you can have a nice, soft song playing in the background.

Imagine you're a star in the sky. And now imagine how big you are, what shape you've got, how do you radiate the light, what colours do you radiate, do you also create sounds as well? Just imagine yourself being this star.

Then imagine God has placed you in a certain spot in the sky. You are amongst other stars. Notice how big they are, what their light is like and anything else you want to notice at this moment.

Now imagine that it is night time and people are staring at the sky. They notice a sky full of stars. They can't tell them apart. What do you believe they think about you? About the other stars close to you? About stars generally? About the sky?

Now imagine that God comes back to you and gives you advice: what will HE tell you?

Allow for the words to come. Don't stop them. Allow for the vision to continue for as long as it wants. And when you open your eyes, write down the advice you've received.

Whichever tool you will use, just take time to write down all the advice you get.

And then make the decision to move forward. Even if you don't know what that looks like at the moment. The guidance and help will come just as I have mentioned in the previous chapter.

CHAPTER 5.4

FAITH

"When you come to the end of all the light you know, and it's time to step into the darkness of the unknown, faith is knowing that one of two things shall happen: either you will be given something solid to stand on or you will be taught to fly."

~ Edward Teller

I can't count the times when I have just taken the plunge, and if I were to have really thought about it beforehand I would have decided that it was stupid and have done nothing.

Like deciding to leave home when I was just sixteen. I had nowhere to go. No money to my name. No job. Not enough knowledge to get any ... nor the right age, not for my country at that time. Yet the decision was staring at me: simple and still like the surface of undisturbed waters. I had no time to weigh it in, understand consequences or analyse risks. All I knew was that in order to be safe I needed to run away. It was after a long night of beatings. My brothers were wandering around the streets at 3 am in the morning. I was sheltering at a neighbour's. The police found my brothers and because they weren't looking like punks, they stopped to ask them what was happening and why were they not at home sleeping? They fearfully started telling the police what was happening at home.

At that time, in my country, police were not allowed to intervene in family matters, even if someone were to scream 'help, he's killing me'. So they needed someone to call them and that was where I got involved. So when my brothers showed up at the neighbour's door, I asked the police explicitly for their help telling them we were in danger.

All of us gingerly entered our home with the police alongside us. I can't describe what exactly happened then, it was such a traumatic blur. At the same time, I was aware of how serious this was. I felt terror pulsing through my veins and by the venomous expression on my father's face, I saw how personally he took the intrusion. He even started calling me vicious names in front of the police in a snarly voice and one of the police men asked him if this is the way he normally spoke to his daughter. To which I intervened: "Wait, this isn't even the beginning of it. He calls me an animal, someone who will end up giving head in the street as her career. And wait 'til he stomps on me with his feet". Everything began to spill out, unleashed after being silenced and held in for such a long time.

The adrenaline rush kicked in. I could sense the terror and hate on my father's face. But he had to calm himself down as the police were very crafty with the way that they approached him. I can't remember anything they said as they spoke. All I remember was the fact that I knew I had betrayed my father and that I would face the consequences but, at the same time, I knew I'd stopped him from something more horrible.

This was the start of what turned into me 'divorcing' my father and freeing my mum and my brothers from this toxic environment.

Instead of going straight to school that morning, I went to the hospital to get my wounds checked out, now that they were fresh. The 'certificate' the hospital released showed that the beating I had the night before required seven days of hospitalisation. With this proof, I went to my school and talked to my principal. I told her that I wanted to sue my father and start legal proceedings. The staff could all see my bruises, and witnessing the shock on my teacher's faces, only made me more certain of how wrong all this was.

Everyone, absolutely everyone, came together to help me. The school's head teacher helped me to get a place in a hostel belonging to the high school I was studying at. Until it was organised I stayed with a friend. The teachers had a discussion and sent me to a prosecutor for me to start sharing what had happened. They also collected some money together to help me for the few days until we had a clearer picture of the outcome. In the meantime, my father vowed that I could return home, and I did for a short time, until he started with the threats again and that's when I left for good. By this time everyone knew what was happening so they were ready to provide the place in the hostel and give me free lunches and support.

I knew this wasn't a permanent solution. And I really did not know what would happen, my life, although chaotic before, now felt even more uncertain. I just took each step as it came.

The providence was with me every step of the way.

To be completely honest with you, I did not expect the support. Not even now, when thinking back, I just don't know how it happened. What did I do to deserve all of that and how did I get them to listen to me? Tears move down my face as I am writing these words. And it's hard to explain. At that time everything just came to me. I wasn't aware of what I was doing, but I can share the feeling. It was like everything just became silent around me. There was quiet in my head, quiet in my body, like I couldn't feel, see, think or experience anything. It was just me and my prayer: "God please help me!"

That's all that I can remember. It must have been that, in a moment of despair and surrender, I'd connected to that true essence of divine light within me that wanted to survive and shine. Once we had connected everything disappeared. There was nothing. From that nothing, the idea appeared; just leave!

It was easy in the moment, when everything became quiet, but acting on it didn't stay the same. I still had to face challenges and overcome them. One in particular stands out. It was when I had to deal with the Romanian authorities for suing my father.

"YOU! You want to sue your father?"

I could hear the prosecutor's judgement in his voice. I knew one thing only: that wasn't right.

"Does my father have the right to kill me?" I replied.

At which point he stared at the ground, then handed me a blank piece of paper and told me to file a complaint.

Even then, there was another person who was put on my path and showed up at the right time; a policeman. This man helped me to draft the complaint. I shared with him what happened and then he dictated to me what to write. And he helped me file it properly.

I had no reason to believe that all of these acts of help and kindness would happen. Hell, I did not even know there was such a thing as a prosecution. I knew about the police. I knew of lawyers, but these people I had no awareness of at all.

That's pretty much how the universe responds when you act from a place of sheer faith. Solutions just appear out of nowhere. People show up from nowhere who are ready to jump in to support you. Suddenly everything seems to just fall into place in a very inexplicable way. Quite amazing if you allow it.

The more I practiced this connection to my higher self and hearing that silence within, the more I learned to lean in and have faith. Trusting enough to let go of the expectation of how things will turn out, and sitting with the uncertainty of all the things that I don't know about and can't possibly figure out in due time.

The more I experienced this practice, I received what you might call a miracle. I know this initial miracle wouldn't have happened if I hadn't made the decision to leave and have faith that God would help me.

Our everyday lives are filled with miracles. We just don't see them unless they come in such an inexplicable way. The more we rationalise why things happened in a certain way, or what science claims to be responsible for, the more we move away from God and life's miracles which means the more we move away from faith.

We do not need to have science tell us how long a pregnancy takes to reach full term, and if we are carrying a healthy baby in our tummy by attending ultra-sound scans. It's good that we can explain things, but we then rely on using those explanations as truths. And we forget that the baby will be birthed into the world with or without the medical assistance.

This has been playing out in society for more than a million years. We have learned to lean more on our analytical brain and only trust what we can see with our eyes. We forgot about faith. However, faith is what allows your body to know how to breathe, how to regulate its temperature, how to create the sleep cycles and everything else that makes our bodies function. Faith is what makes flowers bloom and the other miracles of nature we witness. And so on and so forth.

Faith is what keeps this universe together and all of us united as ONE.

Tapping into faith is available to everybody. We are all born with it. From when we are babies, we have an unwavering faith that we will be taken care of. Think of the helpless baby crying in a cot – relying on the adults around them for their every single basic need. And that's when we grow the most and the fastest. Isn't it interesting? What if we actually lived our lives more in faith, than in understanding and the scientific explanation of things? Maybe we could grow further, faster?

The easiest and fastest way for me to be more invested in faith is through meditation. I usually listen to tracks that help to set my mind in delta/theta waves. It stops the thinking and the need to rationalise everything. It helps me to then focus a lot on the situation that's causing me fear without feeling all of the overriding emotions creating havoc. And, while in meditation, I allow myself to imagine the situation resolving itself miraculously. I play the movie in my mind with the 'happily ever after' scenarios repeatedly, until I feel no emotions at all. I've watched with the mind's eye until I am indifferent to whichever way it will go. I don't know how this happens. But it just does.

From that place of trust I ask myself what I want to do about it. Usually the answers appear very 'loudly' as there is no other thought present to cause distraction. And that's how you know that you have the answer. There is a 'silence' in thoughts as well as in emotions.

It's really that feeling from the quote I've started the chapter with. If you can imagine it and feel it in your body, that's what it will feel like when you've tapped into your higher self and come to an answer from a place of faith.

I would encourage you to practice moments of complete silence every day. You will get to experience the feeling of what that feels and looks like. If you find meditation is not easy for you, you can start with the Headspace app. It's a very powerful and practical tool if you can stick to it daily.

https://www.headspace.com/

CHAPTER 5.5

SURRENDER

"The moment of surrender is not when life is over, it's when it begins."
~ Marianne Williamson

Asking for guidance, receiving it from a place of faith and taking inspired action on that nudge sounds a lot easier said than done. As humans with active minds, it requires a degree of surrendering to whatever might come your way.

Every time you need to surrender you will feel like you are dying, literally. Your whole stomach will turn upside down and you'll feel like you're about to have a panic attack. You will feel like you're being stretched from all corners of your being. It's unmistakable ... you won't be able to escape it. It's like the calm before the storm, only the other way around. In the case of the storm, you know that everything being calm alerts you to seek shelter.

In the case of you surrendering to the outcome, feeling tense before your resolution will alert you to acknowledge that you are about to have a major breakthrough. In a way, it should be comforting to know that the key to unlocking where you are at right now is down to you surrendering and knowing that you will be okay. I say it should be, because in those moments you won't be able to feel it. But at least make a mental note that when you notice your whole being about to break, that this is what's actually happening. The mind loves to know 'what's happening', so it doesn't freak out, but it only serves to add more pressure to the issue which was already difficult to go through.

Remember in the previous chapter on Faith, I mentioned about how I play a movie in my head with things turning out so beautifully and that I play it over and over again until all of the emotion disappears? Part of that process is to also allow for the 'bad' stuff you fear will happen, to happen.

Then imagine a positive come back to that. Imagine this scenario: you have an argument with your husband about money and you are afraid that if you keep pushing for getting what you want then he will leave you. Firstly, imagine how you would obtain the money in miraculous ways. And without forcing the process, the mind will still bring up the fear of losing the husband. Then imagine what would be a miraculous outcome for you. It might be that you finally find the right argument to convince him, and then he will be so grateful that you have. Or it could be that you find another husband quicker, which lets you have whatever you want, whenever you want it.

The key here is to play full out. And don't create any limits such as – 'this or that will never happen.' That's the whole point of imagining it. You can create it in any way with no bounds.

Now, the mind will play tricks and other objections will surface. If you deeply allow, your mind will highlight to you all of your fears and doubts about the situation at hand. But if you stick with the exercise you will reach the point there's going to be nothing left.

And then you can ask the killer question: what shall I do next?

If you feel your stomach clench ... do more work. If it's quiet and the mind doesn't go spiralling off again with all the things that could go wrong, you've reached the point of surrendering.

All you have to do is act on the guidance.

Just so you know:

You will be okay whether your parents love you or not.
You will be okay whether people hate you or love you.
You will be okay whether you fail or pass the test.
You will be okay whether you get fired or not.
You will be okay whether you lose all your money or not.
You will be okay whether your children hate you or not.

You will be okay whether all your attempts to have a business turn out successful or not. You will be OKAY no matter what!

Whether the outcome is positive or negative, (and that is reliant on the meaning that you give it anyway) you will still be okay.

A tool to use here that will ease your way to surrendering is to release yourself from the dilemma of either this or that thinking/black or white thinking and introduce at least one other way of looking at it.

For example, if something happened at work and the only possible outcome you see is either you quit or they fire you. Brainstorm what other alternatives there could be? Maybe move to a different department? Something else?

It's usually the black and white thinking that many of us are hard wired into using as our norm, that makes us struggle with the ability to surrender and to visualise positive outcomes all of the time. That's why I asked you to think of 'miraculously' solving the situation in your visions.

There was this one time where I was very stressed-out at work. Every day felt to me like it was a big trial which could potentially lead to me getting fired. As I was on my way to work this day, all I could hear in my head were the repetitive words of: 'I need a new job! I need a new job!'

Quitting, with nothing else lined up was simply not an option. Then as I left the tube and was climbing the stairs to exit out of the station, there was a blackboard I noticed on the sidewalk. I had never seen it before, nor since that day. On that board it said: "YOU DON'T NEED A NEW JOB!" I passed it by and kept repeating to myself: "You don't need a new job, you don't need a new job" until it hit me – "OMG I don't need a NEW job!"

And then I said: "Okay God, if you believe I don't need another job I will take your advice. However, from this day onward, I will turn this job into the job that I do want and everything else I will simply not be bothered with. And if that will get me fired it will be on you!"

And I went on and did exactly that. Within the space of a few months, I had turned things around completely. I left that company a year later as a winner, being rewarded and publicly acknowledged for my work. I still can't explain how that happened, except that I had surrendered completely to whatever would come as a result of showing up the way that I wanted and nothing else. You see, up until that point it never crossed my mind that I could make my job my own and it wasn't down to the job description or my manager's expectations of me. It was mine.

Before that occasion, whenever there was a conflict between what I felt was right to do and what other people in my company thought, the only way I knew how to solve it was: either they leave or I did. It was a very rigid way of thinking and very prone to bring so much misery into my life.

The second that I created a third option, then it became a choice, I felt freer, and with that choice was the power to surrender.

Always know that you have a choice and if it's not an obvious one, then make one up, a MIRACULOUS one! You will be amazed with what will happen afterwards.

With all the work that I have done on myself and the immense growth I've experienced, I am still amazed and puzzled by how I managed to turn that extremely political situation around; something that not even my manager's manager could make happen.

Somehow I did, and it was all because I surrendered.

CHAPTER 5.6

INTEGRITY

"Nothing is impossible – the word itself says, "I'm possible!"

~ Audrey Hepburn

Surrendering to one course of action or another is never a singular choice or action.

It was not enough to decide that I would create myself the job that I wanted only on that day. With every situation at work, every day, I had to choose to respond differently. I had to decide if it was aligned with my new-found resolution or not and consciously choose time and time again to do something different, knowing that it had the potential to get me fired. But God had different plans, so I had to give the new path a chance.

You can't go after the life you dream of by testing the waters with your toes. You need to take the plunge right here and right now! There is no: "let's see what happens and then make the decision. It's more like, make the decision and then it will happen."

I remember this memory as if it was yesterday. It was a time after I had my children and they were around eighteen months old. I was still living in Romania and suffering from depression, not being able to recognise myself. I felt like a failure on all of my plans. Until the moment I got down onto my knees and asked God for his help. It was the time I had begun to understand I needed to do more work on myself and that I needed help.

And I prayed: "God, oh dear God, please help me! I promise I will never, ever, ever stop working on myself. Whatever it takes, I will do it. Just cut me some slack here please. Give me a hand and I promise I will do whatever it takes."

I kept my promise and I will never break it. Even today, as I am writing this, I am enrolled in a program to help me with developing my mindset further. I commit to putting myself in those environments which challenge me to grow, no matter what level I will be at, or how many achievements I've accomplished. This is a non-negotiable for me. That's the power of a promise. That's how it looks being in integrity with yourself.

As opposed to the black and white thinking I was referring to in the previous chapter, and the various options that you have, in this case, the decision is the most powerful tool in the universe. As when it's made, and it's with absolute integrity with the power behind it, there is no doubt as to what is going to happen.

It's literally like a key turning at the right moment in the corresponding keyhole. You see all of the moving pieces lining up in order to get you to the desired outcome. But with this, there is no grey area. It's either you've made a decision to which you commit to fulfil or you haven't. There are no 'buts' or 'what ifs', or 'only ifs' ... it's like a COMMAND.

Think of it like this. When you get into a cab, do you tell your driver: "maybe take me to Central Plaza, or if it might take longer, maybe take me to the other side of the city?"

What would a sane person answer to that? They'll probably ask: "Lady, where do you want to go - to Central Plaza or to Grand Union Station?"

You have to give very clear instructions and then stick to them.

Of course there is always an option to change your mind. But then don't wonder why you didn't get to Central plaza, if midway, you've changed your mind and instructed your driver to go in the opposite direction, and then proceed to blame him because he didn't go to Central Plaza in the first place and because he didn't ignore the second commands.

You can't do this. Not if you really want to get what you want. You can consider Central Plaza your destination right now, whatever that may mean for you - financial freedom, happiness, health or other, and then give clear instructions and stick to them.

Your sabotaging patterns might want to derail you, trying their best to convince you that there is plenty of time and that you can turn around for a while, or that you don't actually have to do anything. If it's meant to be yours, it will be yours. True - but only if you go for it. You have to meet God halfway there. And you can't do that by using wishy washy tactics and fumbling your way there. One day saying one thing and the next saying and doing the opposite. That won't get you anywhere and you will be tested over and over again on your declarations. And you will need to reaffirm them absolutely every time.

You might think "what if it's the wrong decision?" Usually everyone has that doubt right after they have just made a choice. It's the Saboteur. We all have it. The way to distinguish between making a bad decision and the doubting sabotage thought that comes right after you've made a decision is this: When the decision has been made there is stillness and clarity in the moment that it came as a thought. It's that moment of clarity I've described in the previous two chapters. If this moment comes then the decision has been made. If you haven't yet reached this moment, it just means that you need to work through it further until you're ready to surrender to one course of action.

If you did make the right decision, everything that happens after to challenge the validity of your decision is plain and simple fear. You went through a process to get to the moment of clarity. That is undeniable and indisputable. All that this means is that you need to start slaying the monsters of your mind which try very hard to keep you where you are at and not change a thing. And this is why, if your resolve is weak, you will never win when this happens. The only way to push through this fear is if your commitment to get through with it is set to one hundred percent. When you've burnt the boats, there is no other option but to take the island!

What promise will you make to yourself first and foremost today? Right now?

What promise will you make to your God/Creator that will help you to be happy and free and have what you always dreamed of having?

What's your version of burning the boats to get to the life that you want? Right now? How can you burn the boats?

Write your answers on post-it notes and have them displayed in multiple places. This way, your subconscious gets programmed each time you notice them. Put them on your phone's screen saver, on your laptop, in your bedroom and everywhere you are bound to see them.

You can also send your promise to me: <u>contact@laurahurubaru.com</u>. Use the subject line: My promise to myself is:

I've learned that it's easier to disappoint ourselves. But when we make a promise to somebody else, especially if they are strangers, that bond is a lot stronger. Send your promises my way and use that as a powerful leverage to propel you to your desired destination.

CHAPTER 5.7

COMMITMENT

"Motivation is what gets you started. Commitment is what keeps you going."

~ Jim Rohn

The truth is very simple; the only difference between the women who get what they want and those who don't is their level of commitment. Nothing else. They are no smarter, brighter, luckier or more attractive than you. They don't have a rich husband ... none of that. They've just decided that they will go and get what they want, whatever it takes! They made a promise to themselves that they won't break come hell or high water.

If you are like I was ten years ago, I know these three words: **whatever it takes**, will scare the shit out of you. As based on your previous experience, which probably wasn't that positive, whatever it takes means walking through hell and fire.

But it's not that. Whatever it takes, when it comes to you finding your purpose and living the life you deserve is not more hell and fire, it's a different path to follow. It's actually unlearning that. And moving against fear all the time. Against all of the constructs you've built to keep yourself safe. Those are the real aspects of hell and fire. When you let go of them you find more peace and love.

But it has to be whatever it takes, it starts and ends there. And with our minds being as they are, it's easier said than done as we are all addicts to our emotions and to the chemicals we release in response to fear, that our brains experience a lot of the time. And even with all of our good intentions, we will still sabotage our happiness and success.

What does commitment really look like? Well let's do a small exercise:

Let's imagine you want to be able to create a life where you don't depend on a boss to dictate your schedule. That you have the freedom to move around and travel, and you can also be available for your family while building your career. And let's assume you're looking to always create a form of passive income so you become financially independent as well.

Let's say I ask you how committed you are to yourself to achieve these results in the next five years or so.

And you say 100%. Then answer this:

On a scale from one to ten, one being a person who said that they want to lose weight but with the next chance they get they are raiding the fridge, eating cake, and ten being the person who, even throughout Covid, bought an exercise bike or a trampoline and they exercised indoors daily.

Where would you say you are with your level of commitment in terms of putting in the time, the energy and the financial resources to get the help that you need to create these results in your life?

You should have three marks. Write them all down. If they are anything but a ten, the hard cold truth is that you are not really committed to making your dream come true.

And that's the end of it. Any justifications as to why it is not a ten, is your mind convincing you that it's better where you are right now. It's safe. And you don't need to change anything at the moment.

See, while I understand and accept and follow divine timing myself also, this thinking is dangerous because it makes you act as though you have been granted to live a thousand years. Start to challenge that voice.

Challenge the voice which says it's okay for you to wait, to take it slow...

Who's saying that? Is it your higher self or is it your saboteur?

If you were to be brutally honest with yourself, what is the truth?

I really love Stephen Covey and his principle to "Start with the end in mind". That's where he asks people to imagine their own funeral, and notice who will be present and what will be said about themselves.

I'd ask you to consider that if you were to die tomorrow, would you still be happy with what the inner voices are telling you? Or would you make a new decision? Would you be determined to find a way and not stop until you do? Be honest. And then go back and look at your daily actions. Do they reflect this truth? Or not so much?

I am curious what your answer will be. That's going to determine if and when your dream will come true for you.

The more truthful you can be with yourself, the better chances you will get to reach your desires. And this ties in with the previous chapter. You can't change your life if you keep lying to yourself.

If you feel like you're not there yet, I believe you have not yet figured out your big WHY. That in itself can take people a lifetime. And it's understandable that when you lose the purpose and the reason for being alive, "whatever" mindset action will do. But the only reason you might have ended up in this situation is because you allowed yourself to be pushed around, by not sticking to what you said you will do and breaking your promises more than you make them.

Let's get some honest truth from you today:

What is it you truly want out of this life?

If absolutely anything was possible and you have a magic wand, what would the perfect life for you look like?

Why do you want the things that you want?

What happens if you don't get them? How would that make you feel?

I will let you in on a little secret; if the pain of not having isn't bigger than the discomfort of making it happen, it will NEVER happen.

I wished someone had told me these things when I was still thinking and behaving from a victim's identity, when I believed that something was wrong with me and that's why I didn't get what I wanted and probably never would. But I didn't.

So if you're reading this, I urge you to take this chapter very seriously and really put in the time and effort into thinking long and hard about the tough choices that you have. In ten years from now when you will look back, you will thank yourself for doing so.

Don't just brush it off and say "yeah, yeah". Your life depends on this. So follow the instructions and do the homework suggested!

There is a process that Tony Robbins shares in his UPW events. It's called the Dickens process. Find the space and time to do it. If you are not on the floor crying your heart out while doing it, you're not doing right.
https://www.youtube.com/watch?v=8awWbuFQL2Q

Do it as seriously as you can and as often as you need to, until you can feel you've reached a ten out of ten on your commitment to putting in the time, the energy and the money to make it all happen.

Imagine you're one year ahead and your life has dramatically changed since you've done these exercises. And then write a letter to your old self to thank her for taking the action and making the decision to change her situation.

Describe what your life looks like now because she decided!

And because she put in the work. Tell her all the details!

Don't leave anything out.

Sign it.

And read it every day.

You can also record yourself reading it and listen to it daily.

You will need it!

CHAPTER 5.8

ACKNOWLEDGE YOURSELF

"A journey of a thousand miles begins with a single step."

~ Chinese proverb

Changing habits that have been with you for a lifetime is hard work. It requires ongoing discipline and commitment. You have to accept and understand that by the time you become a new woman, the old you will still be there. You need to celebrate and acknowledge every small step that you take to improving your life, otherwise you will quit too soon.

I see this all of the time: women having real difficulties acknowledging themselves. God knows I suffer from this too and try hard every day to value myself and see myself in a higher light. I guess it's a curse women seem to carry, especially the ones who suffered any kind of abuse. Somewhere along the way, in our nurturing nature, we have learned that caring, loving and being there for another human being is 'nothing'. It is our duty as mothers/daughters/sisters. We took this form of self-sacrifice to not being able to see the difference between loving unconditionally and sacrificing our wellbeing and lives for others.

When you love someone you will know that sometimes the best thing to do for them is to let them go and help them to stand on their own two feet. That's something I understood from a young age and it landed me in trouble because my parents did not see it the same way.

When I started school and didn't know how to solve a problem or do the homework and asked for help at home, all I got in return was: "You should already know this! What did you do in class when the teacher was teaching you this?"

And if I wasn't able to solve it myself I would get beaten. Quickly I learnt to not go and ask for help and often ended up waking in the middle of the night with the solution. But then my brothers started school. Suddenly I was the one to have to help them with their homework, and if I wouldn't do it, I was told that I was mean, heartless and a sister who didn't care. I remember many times like these. One of my brothers would not know how to solve a problem and they would come asking for help. I would ask what they'd tried already and the answer was always nothing because they didn't know where to begin to solve it. I would send them back to start somewhere and then to explain to me where they get stuck so I could help. And then they could go back again and finish it on their own. They would cry and tell our parents that I refused to help. Then my parents would beat the shit out of me, but still I would not budge. After all, I had no help from them when I was in a similar position. But that's not why I refused so strongly to do it. It was because I knew that it wasn't really helping. When it came to them having to sit the tests and exams they wouldn't be equipped to solve those problems then either. And I wouldn't be there to do it for them. So they needed to learn to do it on their own. That's the genuine help they needed in the long term.

Of course it didn't help my parents but I know that every one of my brothers are where they are right now because I chose not to 'help' them in the way my parents thought I should. In the way they thought a 'good' sister should do. I helped them in a way that I knew was sustainable for their long term success. Plus, if I were to give in to their requests I would have ended up doing everyone's homework all of the time – including my own!

And when it came for me to be acknowledged, forget it - it was like asking for their teeth. They just could not see it. And I started believing it too - that it wasn't smart what I was doing ... that I was not that smart... that I am just selfish and only looking out for myself.

Since it was so painful, I started believing that I was mean and uncaring to myself too. At least I didn't have to deal with them being unfair because that was "the truth". Right?

From this rather harsh foundation, I've trained myself to not seek or accept recognition or acknowledgement from anyone else. Not that I didn't need it, but because it was a way for me to cope with people not seeing who I truly was... to the point that I didn't know who I was. I couldn't see how capable I am. I couldn't accept this version of me - resourceful, kind and loving, that I was, because I chose to avoid the pain of having parents who didn't see me or appreciate me. It was safer to lie to myself that I deserved that judgement.

We do this all the time. We dress up the lies and make them the truth, keeping the lies festering and growing in grotesque ways. That's why sorting out your integrity is a must. You can't do this work by dressing up lies as truths and shutting the truths away because they are too painful to look at.

We all do this to some extent. In your case, it might be your spouse or friends who told you who you are. It may even be a part of yourself which is convinced that you are not worthy and there is nothing of value you can offer to the world; a part that dictates that you shouldn't be having these wild dreams. You have no traits or skills to qualify you enough. You are a nobody...

If you don't learn anything from this book, but you take this single one thing and practice it daily, I promise it will change your life forever. One day you will wake up to the beautiful being that you are and understand how much BS you believed and told yourself for a lack of better tools.

Right now, take some time with yourself and start journaling:

- **Think of times where you succeeded against all odds: what were they and what three things can you acknowledge yourself for?**
- **If you asked your best friend about the top three qualities they see in you that they believe are priceless, what are they?**
- **If you were to be completely honest and loving towards yourself what are the top three qualities you love about yourself?**
- **Daily do this, either in the morning before you start your day or in the evening: ask yourself: what can I acknowledge myself for yesterday/today?**
  Don't move on until you find three reasons for which you should acknowledge yourself.

When you learn to do this, little by little, you will start seeing the progress you are making. And this is huge. A lot of people quit in the middle of their diet for example because they don't see results fast enough, so in their impatience, they decide it's not working.

For example, writing this book was extremely challenging for me for two reasons: I had to go back and revisit some memories that I thought best to be left behind. And second, I am not a writer. This is my first ever book. My old and entrenched perfectionistic patterns gave me a hard time to even try, as no matter what I would do, it wasn't going to be good enough. How can it be? If I have never done it before why do I expect it to be great? But then if it's not great, why am I writing it? Why do I even bother?

Does this sound familiar?

Well, the truth was I made a promise to myself (chapter 5) in that I will publish my book this year (2021). And then I hired someone to coach and mentor me through (chapter 6). But even with this support, I still had troubles getting myself to write. I would be exhausted by the time I wanted to start writing anything. And then I would keep repeating to myself: "Just one sentence. That's it. Don't look for perfection, just progress. Focus on adding just one more line. Even if it's just one line, it is still one line more than yesterday. And if you keep doing this, without realising, it will be done".

The funny thing was that even if I said to myself every morning before I started writing: "just one line", I would end up writing a whole chapter or two. I did this a few times and with the encouraging feedback that I received from my mentor, I spent less and less time and energy into getting me to do it.

So now you can read it! 😁

I had to create the discipline to put myself in front of the computer daily and write at least one sentence. And my reward was the hot chocolate from Starbucks, which I absolutely love and makes me feel good every time I take a sip.

Strive for progress every day and then acknowledge it every time it happens, no matter how small that is.

Here are some ideas to acknowledge and celebrate yourself with every step you take:

- **Register for a class or workshop about something that interests you, just for fun.**
- **Enjoy a nice meal alone or with a friend or loved one.**
- **Listen to music you love and sing or dance like no one is watching.**

- **Buy yourself some flowers or a plant.**
- **Draw, take an art class, create some art.**
- **Brainstorm your own.**

CHAPTER 5.9

FORGIVENESS

"To forgive is to set a prisoner free and discover that the prisoner was you."
~ *Lewis B. Smedes*

The more that you follow and implement the steps I've laid out in this book, you'll come to realise and awaken more and more to the simple yet painful truth; it was you all along. Or better yet, it was your mind that created all of the situations and the reactions to them. And made up all of the stuff about everything and everyone, including yourself.

And now, not only do you understand where you've made the mistakes, but you will also understand how many people you've hurt in the process because you didn't trust them, pushed them away and you found and chose fights everywhere. And more importantly, you will realise the pain that you put yourself through.

Waking up to the truth, although a very cathartic experience, is also very painful.

The next key thing you need to learn how to do, and to do it consistently, is to forgive yourself and others for all of the past hurt. Whether you are aware of it or not, forgive anyway.

And the process starts with yourself.

If we share similar journeys, and I believe that we do if you're still here reading, then you will be the last one to be let off of the hook for a mistake. If another person wronged you, you will be quick to find reasons to defend them - but if it's you that you need to forgive, that's a whole different story. When it comes to you: you should have known better! You should have done things differently and so on and so forth, says the inner critic.

When it comes to letting go and moving on, even though you put in the inner work to change and heal ... you may not be able to. And that is because a part of you, on some level, cannot forgive you for the role that you played in that situation and for the mistakes you made for the things that you didn't know. And that stings. That's where the pain shifts to unbearable, as whether you liked it or not, it's you who is responsible. You need to make peace with that fact and you need to accept you won't be able to effectively move on unless you forgive yourself.

I find this very hard to do myself as well. Somehow I 'deserve' special treatment, which is nothing else but me beating myself up right down to the bone. Through many painful experiences, I've learned to trick my mind to be able to do it. The tactic I use is to imagine that it was one of my children making that mistake. If they were to speak to me about it and say sorry - what would I reply? Would I forgive them?

So far I have never had a situation whereby they have made a mistake and I have said: "No! You don't deserve to be forgiven! You should have known better!"

I am pretty sure that it will work for you too. If you were to think of your child, or a loved one if you do not have children, doing those 'terrible things' you are struggling to let yourself off the hook from, I am certain that you would forgive that person.

What is it then about you that makes what you did unforgivable?

Usually nothing. It's just the entrenched pattern of beating yourself up which gets a thrill every time it has the opportunity to do so. It's your mind telling you that you need to be punished to make it right. When did that ever make things right? Never! Only unconditional love has the power to really heal and fix things and past mistakes. Unconditional love doesn't call for punishment, it does call for forgiveness though.

One simple and easy to remember tool to help you with this, is the ancient Hawaiian "Ho'oponopono prayer".

It goes like this:

"I am sorry.
Please forgive me.
Thank you.
I love you."

When I practice it, I tend to think of all of the parties involved in the situation including the part in me that created it, or the part in me that got hurt and can't get past the hurt.

And I keep repeating this prayer to each party over and over again until I feel at peace, and there is no longer any tension, nor tears which need to be released.

And then I change it a little bit and repeat the process again.

"I forgive you.
Thank you.

I am sorry.

I love you."

It then represents a reply coming from the other person of acceptance. And I do that with the parts of myself as well, and repeat until I feel the emotional charge is no longer there.

Sometimes, when the memory is particularly painful and too active, I practice it through writing it out. As it helps me to slow down my thinking and it allows for the tears and the pain to come out. I don't try to stop it or make it go away. Au contraire, I am amplifying it to make sure that everything is purged out of my system and then it's complete.

So now, you try:

Think back to a time where you made a terrible mistake that you have not yet completely forgiven yourself for.

Journal everything in relation to the situation, what was it, what happened, what did you do, how you have contributed to it and so on.

Then ask yourself what you need to forgive yourself for in relation to this situation, and then follow the process I've just described.

When you're done and feel at peace or exhausted, write down how that made you feel. Look for ways that it helped. Then you can search for all the other reasons you need to do this.

When you manage to release these burdens from your body and psyche in this way, you will feel like a newborn baby again.

Try it and let me know how it went for you!

CHAPTER 5.10

LOVE YOURSELF

"There is no love without forgiveness, and there is no forgiveness without love."
~ *Bryant H. McGill*

I believe this to be such a huge chapter for the whole of humanity that it needed its own dedicated space here. I feel that all of our mishaps, all of the conflicts internally and externally, all of the lack in the world is due to the fact that we don't know what love truly is. And we don't know how to love ourselves first and foremost.

As I mentioned in the chapter on Courage, I could not have recognised that the situation I was in wasn't healthy, I could not have left home and taken life into my own hands had I not loved myself enough ... and if I'd have stayed longer, I might have ended up dead.

At the same time, I could not have made peace that my father isn't the father that I needed nor my mother, unless I could forgive myself for not being the 'daughter' everyone was expecting me to be at that time in my home country.

Somehow love and self-love is so alien to us that it feels weird to honour it and then we cover it with a lot of guilt and shame because it doesn't show up in the way people expect it to show up.

I mentioned about self-sacrifice already and the difference between doing things for people instead of helping them learn how to do it for themselves - but society is built in such a way that even the most noble of causes, if you really look deeply, stem from a place where people wished things would have been different for them. That somehow things would have been easier, that somebody could have arrived sooner to save them. There is also a huge difference between doing it because it's the reason why God put you on this planet, or because of the wounded side of you that didn't get the help they wished they had.

Without turning this into a witch hunt, there are plenty of books on this topic revealing how the systems we have built are in fact built from a place of powerlessness by a person who has not healed themselves, so they create something which views other people as powerless. They then help to perpetuate the same things that keep themselves and others from getting what they want/need.

There's a lot to be done in this area globally as I already mentioned, and this book alone won't change that. But I am hoping that with every person who reads it and chooses to live in unconditional love, then there is hope that one day we will all be there.

My aim is for this book to shift something within you and that when you have healed past your wounds and negative situations, you will take the empowered direction of helping others. A way that presumes that people are strong enough and they will find their way. They don't need someone else doing it for them. This never works. Look how hard it is to beat any kind of addiction. It doesn't help unless the person wants to take the responsibility to change and they feel empowered to do so. As long as they count on somebody else to do it they will never heal themselves.

Ensure that you don't do it for the powerless part within you, but for the victor in the other person. How do you know that you have the unconditional love for yourself as well as for the other person? There is no judgement or need to understand why you are the way you are, or why the person is the way they are, or why you're doing what you're doing. I use the same example with the child. If one day your child throws a tantrum, would you start questioning him why or would you try and comfort him?

The way to tell whether you are in judgement or are showing up as unconditional love is to examine your questions. How many questions are about you understanding the situation so you can fix it? And how many are there out of love to help the person to make the right choices on their own? The one singular question there should be in your head though which can't be mistaken, is: "What would love do? What does unconditional love require me to do in this instance?" And see what the answer is.

Don't kid yourself thinking you know better. You don't!

I don't know now what is best for you. I write this book in the hope that there is something that will be triggered within you that will see you go on your own path. However, that is up to you and your creator. It might be that you throw this book in the trash bin, because that only means it's not the right time, or meant for your journey. And that's okay. That's the beauty of this world. That's why we are all unique. That's why we are such amazing and powerful beings. Each path is literally a path perfect for absolutely each and every one. And no one is an expert on yours, but yourself.

Now, things get interesting as it's where integrity plays a big role and where you have to honour your truth. Otherwise you won't be showing love to yourself. Sometimes, there will be people on your path or you will be a part of theirs as a wake-up call. And that wake-up call might come in the form of an unpleasant event. You need to be able to view the negative situations and people in the same way; they are on their path, as you are on your path.

There is a reason why both of you crossed each other's paths, but you can't deny who you are out of fear and thinking that 'it's wrong for the other person'. You have to trust that it was for a reason higher than both of you, and the lessons and the teachers come in many shapes and forms. The only time you would not speak your truth is when you can't see the person's higher self. The one able to make the right choice, even if that time might not be now.

I love this quote so much, I can't stop sharing it. I don't know who said it, but here it goes:

"We cannot force someone to hear a message they are not ready to receive. But we must never underestimate the power of planting a seed."

It's an act of unconditional love to deliver a message that you know is not going to be well received, and also an act of courage.

Another way to spot if you are coming from unconditional love is to see if there is a polarity created: me vs you, white vs. black, right vs. wrong which is pretty much the black and white thinking I was describing in the Surrender to the outcome chapter. The world is much more complex than that with lots of grey.

Another quote on this, from Rumi this time is: "Beyond the field of right and wrong, I will meet you there".

We tend to look at things in black and white and through our own experience lenses. So when we had a similar experience with someone we tend to impose 'our truth' of the matter, telling them what they should do or what they should learn and so on. The truth is ... that was YOUR lesson, YOUR truth needed for YOUR journey. So you can't even begin to compare and think the same applies to them as you don't know their journey. You can't compare two journeys as they are as different as snowflakes are in that no two are alike.

Unconditional love accepts and implies that everything is perfect the way that it is. There are no good feelings or bad feelings, there are no good people or bad people. We all came here to play a role and grow through it. And some of us might have chosen to learn it the easy way, some the hard way. Who are we to say which one it was? Or which one is best?

Unconditional love has no set right outcome. There is no such thing as a 'right' outcome. Each action has an impact and creates a ripple effect in other people's lives and you can never be aware of its extent. If you can place your head on the pillow at night, proud you've done your best, irrespective of what the outcome will turn out to be - you're in love. You're in expansion. You are exactly how God created you to be. And through that co-creation, amazing things will happen. And you might never know about it. And that's okay.

I don't know your religion and this isn't religious, but when I think of unconditional love, I think of Jesus. Not because he 'sacrificed' himself as I don't think that's what he did. I believe he loved people so much, he understood that what he preaches is so unheard of and unthinkable but nevertheless he spoke his truth. And he knew it was the truth. He knew that this is the way. And he knew what would happen and how people would react when exposed to this level of truth and certainty about it.

He had the courage and the integrity to carry himself and the message he believed in, even though he knew it would not be received with booze and crowns and coins. If he would have changed his mind based on what other people would think about him or what he said - we would not speak about him thousands of years later. Plus, we don't know what impact the lack of his message would have been. Maybe we would have still stoned people in the streets, or killed others to right a wrong? Who knows? I don't even want to entertain this thinking. For the purpose of this book, he is the epitome for what integrity, forgiveness and love resembles. Think of him and what he would do or say in a particular situation and let his wisdom come through.

The message is not that you need to get crucified for it. Those were the times then. That was the punishment for speaking and living your truth. There are other tools these days, like social media but still, if you have been put on this planet to deliver a message, no matter how unpopular, you will receive the help you need to succeed.

It's my absolute belief that if we all carried a little bit more love for ourselves in our hearts, we would see less bullying in school, less need for 'being prepared in military fashion', less violence everywhere and more love, peace and harmony. I am a naive person this way. Even knowing that I can't change the world, I know that I can create more love, peace and ease in my life. And that's by keeping doing what I have shared with you already.

CHAPTER 5.11

TIME

"Time is the wisest counselor of all."
~ *Pericles*

There is something puzzling about how people choose to live their lives, and that is their relationship with time.

On one hand I feel that when it comes to their big picture, to the masterpiece of their life, people live their lives as though they will last forever and repeatedly put things onto the back burner. Then, before they know it, life has caught up and they are facing their last days on earth. On the other hand, when it's something very specific that they want, and of a lesser significance, like a better job, a raise, a new partner - they act as if there is no time at all and panic as though the world would come to an untimely end should they not take action. I can't quite put my finger on why it's so twisted, and almost a paradox in terms of it making no sense.

Ideally, you would want someone to treat their life seriously, like there's no tomorrow and you would love nothing more than for them to give their best, for absolutely every second of their waking reality. And when it comes to more trivial things, such as "will she say yes?" or "will I get a 10% discount?" for them to not take more than ten per cent, if even that, up of the space in their mind.

I guess it's down to learning and accepting what is truly important in life. I think we've got our definitions mixed up by the way society brainwashes us.

I, for one, have struggled a lot with "When" questions:
When is it going to be my time?
When will I get what I want?
When will I be happy?

And then I move to the 'Never' brother:
What if I will never be happy?
What if all I want is just a fool's wish?
What if I can never find what I am looking for?

And so on – you can see the picture here.

What about you? How much time do you actually spend in your mind and how much on being present in the moment? I bet most of the time you figure out things to worry about, scenarios that will never happen, fights you will never have...

Meanwhile, the ones who love you are there for you, hoping to see you smiling today. Meanwhile, the people who are there for you hope that you will acknowledge them today. Meanwhile, the whole universe hopes to see you excited that you are alive today.

That's why I like Stephen Covey's approach to life: start with the end in mind, which I described more in the chapter Commitment. It forces you to really think about what matters to you the most and to build your life around these things first and foremost, and not bother about the rest. Ultimately, I think we all want to be loved, to feel loved and know that our lives matter. I believe it's in our nature.

I would like to share a little story with you. I believe this story is the best way to describe the healthy relationship one must have with time.

There was one island which was responsible for holding all of the feelings. Amongst the feelings there was also Love. One day, the island starts sinking, and slowly, one by one, the feelings began to leave the island to find a safe place to be. All except Love, which decided to stay a little bit longer with the island. When there wasn't much left of the island, Love being the last one left, realised it was time for it to go too.

Love saw the Vanity boat coming in their direction and asked for its help to get to safety. Vanity said "Sorry Love. You are too wet for my boat. I can't take you."

Then the Wealth boat showed up and Love asked for help. Wealth said "Sorry Love. There is not much room left for you. I am full of silver and gold. I can't take you."

Then along came Sadness. Love said "Please take me with you!"

Sadness uttered "Sorry Love, I need to be on my own right now."

Happiness didn't even notice Love stranded on what was still left of the sinking island. Then, out of the blue, a boat arrived and took Love to safe land. Love was very surprised as it didn't know who was in charge of the boat. Love was surrounded by a lot of wise silhouettes; including Patience and Wisdom. Love asked "Hey guys - did you see who brought me? Do you know who that was?"

The wise beings all said "What? You don't know who took you?"

Love replied "No! Please tell me!"

The wise beings answered "It was Time! Because only Time knows the true value of Love."

This is a story I heard at one of the events I have attended in the past. I don't know who wrote it and its origin, but it hit me deeply. It still brings tears to my eyes when I think of it.

Also during that event, the coach asked us later on, to imagine that we were Love, and that we were on this sinking island and to visualise for some time which boats came close to our island but didn't take us where we needed to be.

But that wasn't all. The next assignment was to imagine Time coming up to save us. And then to imagine what Time would tell us. We all wrote a letter.

Mine was more of a conversation then a one-sided letter from Time. I want to share it with you as I believe it has an immense power within the message. I hope it will help you to see your journey with time a little more clearly.

Here it goes:

Dear Laura,

Finally I get to sail with you! I am so excited you've made it. I can't tell you how proud I am to see you here now. I've waited for so long for this exact moment. I was so excited looking forward to this moment.

I know it's hard for you to believe this, but I always knew that we would both meet one day. And that together we will make the most important journey of your life. The one you get to recognise yourself and recognise that the Time has come for you to be FREE. And even if you were scared for a while, you've found your way! (as I always knew you would).

I know the Past hasn't been easy on you and you have carried it with you... but that's MY job. I also know that I have been kind to you; look at your face, you have aged so beautifully, you look ten years younger than you are.

Let the Past be with the Past. And trust me, trust that I am taking you where you need to be...

Know now that what once was a hope, a wish, now has come true. Time heals everything. I am now here to wash it all away. Jump onto this boat with me and I'll carry you and all of the things that you want to take with you. Just know, that where we are going, you don't need anything. Everything is perfectly done for you and it's awaiting your arrival. You can have whatever you want though, but know now that it's not needed where we are going.

"Is there anything you would like to bring with you from the Past?"

Me: "Yes, this happy, caring and sensitive child who would light up the room with her smile!"

"Perfect! Anything else?"

Me: "All the lessons I've learned, the hard way, the easy way, in any way, so I can share them with the world!"

"Super! Is that all?"

Me: "And my heart ... I think I've left it somewhere ... I want to take it with me and put it back where it belongs!"

"Awesome! Let's go! Ready?"

Me: "YES!"

Me: "I am scared!"

"I know. If I tell you that you will get everything you want, because I am Time, and I know, would you believe me? Would you trust me to take you there?"

Me: "Yes! And Time, I have changed my mind. I am leaving it all behind - with the exception of my heart. And I am coming with you!"

I jumped on the boat and the Time asked: "What would you like to know?"

Me: "Tell me about the world dear Time, tell me about what you've learned from all your travels."

"Only beautiful things. You will get to see them too, now that you are on this boat with me. Nothing to be afraid of, everything to be excited about!"

ME: "Any wise words?"

"You're smart, you'll figure it out. You always do. You don't need any more advice. Definitely not from me - I am just a silent observer."

This was the end of this conversation. I always go back to visit this; to me and the Time in the boat. Every time I feel like I am not doing what I am supposed to be doing, every time I feel I am 'wasting' time, every time I feel I should push harder - I just go back to this conversation and remember that Time has got my back. And everything unfolds perfectly the way that it should.

And it's time for YOU to jump in the boat too and do this little exercise yourself:

Find some quiet time and space and imagine that you are Love stranded on the island and Time arrives in a boat to save you.

Write down everything that is happening as you would write a screenplay for a scene in a movie. Let your imagination flow and connect to the characters. Picture it in such a way that you can describe it to someone and they can 'see' it too.

Through stories, metaphors, visions, we connect to that powerful part of our brain which is resourceful. Use

it and trust the visions, the words and the feelings that come. They will guide you with your next step.

It's only when you will give this process the time that it needs, that all the tools which I have shared with you, will start working your miracles. You have to allow yourself the time to become this person you were always meant to be. To be able to return to the pure love you once were as a baby.

And when you have managed to do so, the end will not be so scary anymore and the goals will no longer have meaning. You will feel happy however, as you just learned the truth. You ARE LOVE and it took you a while to see it, but you've got there. And you got there with the help of Time.

CHAPTER 5.12

BECOMING/ASCENDING

"Human beings are not born once and for all on the day their mothers give birth to them, but ... life obliges them over and over again to give birth to themselves."
                                    ~ Gabriel García Márquez

It's only by returning to love, by giving yourself the time and space to come home to yourself, that you will find true lasting happiness.

I have shared with you some tools to help you to master yourself, and ultimately take control of your life. Although the truth is one and simple; you get to create the life that you want. You have to be brave enough though to do it from a space of love and trust, rather than from a place of fear, anger and worry.

These days, with so much support out there in the personal and spiritual development world, people are growing a lot faster and in bigger numbers. What once was the 'dark night of the soul' and would happen once in a lifetime, now it can be fast tracked and happen multiple times a year, depending on your soul's mission during these times.

At the time of writing this book, the whole world was in lockdown due to Covid-19. That in itself was a big wake-up call and a catalyst for change for all humanity. We've been given the chance to slow down, to spend more time around our close ones, to think more thoroughly about what we want to do with our lives, about our health, our bodies and our relationships. It's been massive, on a global scale.

And while reading this book might give you an impulse, you might try some things for a few weeks and you might feel better for a while... but changing one's life takes Time, Commitment and Dedication.

The danger I see happening all the time is when people get themselves in a good place and they think they're done. That's when things start getting weird again - to the point that it feels like you're starting all over again with the misery, struggles and unhappiness.

In a way we are like nature. There are seasons to our lives as well. This may sound depressing but the work on yourself never stops. And I wish that I could tell you it gets easier. To some extent it does, as the more that you learn about yourself, the more you master the process and can use the tools I've shared with you to aid that. The more that you grow, the easier it becomes to recognise your sabotaging patterns, the easier it is to get back on track and the shorter you stay in an unpleasant situation.

I can guarantee you, when you've reached that new level and a breakthrough needs to happen, the moments before that are as painful and as real as any other before that. The parts you need to discard to move into the new uplevelled version of you will feel like your soul is dying and being re-born all over again. And it happens quite frequently.

For me right now, every few months I have a moment like this. I don't believe I will reach a point where I can say: "I am done now! I am a complete masterpiece. After all, I made a promise to God to never stop working on myself."

You'll always be a masterpiece in progress and will be experiencing this 'death' multiple times a year, if not on a monthly basis. This is when you have decided to grow fast and that your soul wants to express itself in its purest form possible. I am telling you; the depth to which you feel comfortable to immerse yourself with feeling the pain, is the same level of depth you get to experience happiness, love, and gratitude. Don't be afraid of venturing into the deepest layers of your being - the darker the room, the brighter and bigger the treasure in it.

My dream was to be FREE. Initially, it played out as being free from a job and a fixed schedule. However, the traditional 9-5 became more like 7-7 and it did not feel like living to me. The more I worked on this dream of mine, the more deeply I understood the meaning of FREE. To the point where I chose to be FREE, even from my dream.

To know that whether it happens or not, or if it happens the way I've planned it or not, it doesn't matter. I am still me. Who I am is a lot more important than all of my achievements. To know that I am okay and I always will be okay. That's GOLD. That FREEDOM you feel inside is priceless. If I have to enter back into the dungeons every other month, slay some more scary dragons, and come back victorious to FREE myself even more, I will gladly do it.

It's a never ending story for me. And I seek it. Will you do the same? Will you be someone I'll meet on the path to true FREEDOM? Will I find you there?

In the last chapter, Time, that is all life is - a journey back to one's self, back to Love as you ARE love. And Love, as everything else, has its stages. There will always be a next level, and another next level, until you unite with God and you're back to your divine pure essence.

Until then, you resemble a butterfly in a chrysalis. Did you actually know that butterflies don't have a very long life span? On average, they live for about a month and in that time, aren't they the most joyous thing to observe? See how they make us happy whenever we notice one, fluttering its stunning wings, as it appears out of nowhere and then vanishes as quickly. It can feel sad to us, because we believe it's the end - but what if there's another type of 'chrysalis'? And when they are finished with this stage, they transform into something else, just as exquisite and beautiful as they were before?

I'd like to imagine our existence like that. By peeling off these layers, in time, we become these amazing beings that are pure joy to be around.

And that's what is waiting for you if you decide to take this path and if you have the courage to follow your heart and the commitment to follow through.

CHAPTER 6

SAYING A YES TO YOURSELF

I know it's a lot to take in and by now, I can imagine you've started to be in your head and feel like the journey is overwhelming, if you are anything like I was not long ago.

Worrying when you will have the time to do everything I've shared with you - what if you can't journal when you are at work in the middle of one of your crying episodes or another inconvenient time?

First understand that this process I've shared with you didn't come to me on day one. It came over time, moving from one step to the next. It took me around five years to get my head above the water and then five more to reach a thriving state of being. It might be different for you. It might take you less, it might take you longer. Just remember, everyone's path is different. And it is perfect for the journey you're on.

Secondly, I want you to think about this book like you would consider a cooking recipe. It has to include all of the ingredients, as well as all the steps on how to cook the dish, using different techniques, in order for you to be able to follow and get the same desired result. Right?

So you can see, I could not have shared with you only one step or just brush over them. I had to describe all of them in as much detail as possible so you can follow them and reach your place of harmony that I promised at the start of the book. The only difference between a cooking recipe and this book, is that culinary dishes might take a maximum of a day to prepare (if it's a complex or a sophisticated one), but this process can take a lifetime.

This has both pros and cons. The positive side is that all you need to do right now is to start. Start with something that is on the path of least resistance for you. If it's Awareness go for it. If it's more Self-love that you are drawn to, that's great too.

While I go over them in a sequential order, as you'll understand from the Time chapter, they all work in sync and the process of growing is more circular, like on a 3D spiral. With each spiral you get to revisit some of the early steps and travel much further in depth with them. Do not worry if you can't start with step one. Just start.

Another pro with this approach, based on your soul path and your contract, is that you may discover your own process. Through taking the first step, you may realise that for your journey, it's much more important to go through a self-discovery journey for example, and to focus only on Awareness, until the answer you seek reveals itself and it will guide you somewhere else; to another book perhaps, or a course or a person suitable for that step of your journey. God knows, I've been like a bee jumping from one flower to another in my search for answers. That's not to say that there are chapters more important than others, no, but your path to each and every one of them might be different from mine and that's okay.

The problem with taking longer than just a day, when it comes to our lives, is that it takes years, our whole life literally. It can be hard for you to see the progress and that what you're doing is actually working. You'd have to stick with it for a while, taking that leap of faith, not knowing what's on the other side. At the same time, to not throw this book on a shelf while looking for the next new book title you see on Facebook!

"But Laura, you've got me at chapter one. I want to do everything. I don't even know where to begin, or how I will fit everything in. How shall I do it? I really want to do everything and stick to it for as long as I possibly can."

Great. Follow the same advice; choose one area where you feel you can start implementing right away. Then schedule two hours per week where you review your progress and strategize your next steps. Only do it when you've mastered the first one and that you feel you can add more onto your plate. Most people give up on their goals and plans because they tend to overwhelm themselves. Start small and trust you will get there: "The journey of a thousand miles starts with one single step." Lao-Tzu

Be willing to start small and not see huge shifts overnight. It took you how many years to live with this version of yourself? It will take at least that many to become someone new. Do this regularly at the same day and time if possible so that you train your brain to do that then. When life gets in the way, it will have become a habit, so that no matter what is happening around you, you will still go ahead and do it.

This is the most important time of your life - the one you get to spend with you creating the life that you want. When things move up, you will naturally increase this time and the occurrences of when you strategize and plan for your future.

All good so far?

Awesome.

"What if this doesn't work? How can you be sure it will work for me?"

I don't know you nor can I be sure it will work for you. It's a lot that goes into changing one person's life. What I am sharing with you in this book, is not rocket science. It's not something I have invented. If you study success and people who are even more successful than I am, in one form or another, they are doing the same things. They may have different tools, different routines - but they do practice awareness, learn to master their mind, they choose to continuously grow on a regular basis. It's a lifestyle!

All you have to care about right now is, why do you want to do it in the first place? Isn't that worth a try? And if you gave it a try, isn't it worth sticking with it for a while until you make it work? Until you can make it your own and it becomes second nature?

You tell me! If your why is strong enough, you'll find a way to make it work for you! Got it?

"Laura, it's too hard. I don't know if I can do it."

"Whether you think you can, or you think you can't - you're right." — Henry Ford

Losing weight is hard but so is being overweight.
Being financially free is hard but so is being broke.

1atePROTOTYPE

Feeling happy and joyous is hard but so is feeling miserable.

Choose your hard!

The more you choose the "great" hard, the easier it gets. But you have to do it every time and with every choice.

Being the creator of your life and the master of your destiny is not for the faint of heart. It is for those who really want to unlock their true potential. It is for those who are hungry to get the maximum out of this experience and to grow and be a shining light for others to do the same.

It's for the people who have big hearts because inevitably, when you transcend your limitations, you become a model for other people. It's not for the selfish who only care about themselves.

You have to want to lead the way, and this means that sometimes it will be just you on the path. There will be signposts left by others before you, so you can learn from them while figuring your stuff out also.

You're right, it's not going to be easy.

And be scared about the 'lesser' hard - not about what you need to do to live life on your terms.

"What if I lack the courage to do it?"

We are spiritual beings having a human experience. We are incredible and capable of incredible things.

As Stephen Hawking puts it, we merely inhabit a minor planet in an average star. Everyone has the right to fail and to curl up and sleep all day long for a while. Sometimes, that's exactly what is needed for their healing and their shift to happen.

Think about it. From the cave man days, we are now servicing food to around 7.6 billion people's doors steps. We had to overcome big challenges and dangers to leave behind the 'cave'. If we had lacked courage, we wouldn't be here. We would've starved to death in those caves, rather than be out fighting dangerous animals.

Courage is in our blueprint. Look at a mother when there is a potential danger to her child. There are so many reported "incidents" when people suddenly possess supernatural powers to save another human being from a car accident for example. Our brain and bodies are amazing. They will do whatever it takes to protect us and we can harness this power.

It's already within you. You were designed with it in mind. All you have to do is tap into it and you do that by mastering your mind.

By applying yourself to self-mastery and by doing the work day in and day out!

"What if I don't know how to make decisions... all the decisions I've made turned out shit... how can I trust this time will be different?"

We all make decisions that feel right at the time and then in retrospect we wished we had 'known better'. But that's the thing; if you had known, you would have done it. If you could have done better you would have done already. Whatever was right at that moment for you, was the right thing for the person you were at the time. Spending time beating yourself up for something you did years back, or even days, makes no sense. It's like telling a toddler he didn't know how to tie his laces properly a week ago, when he stumbled on them and fell and bruised his knees. You would not do that!

It's not that different for adults either. We are continuously growing and learning. The stuff only becomes more complicated and difficult - we just need more time to master it. If you've reached the point to understand that the decision you took in the past is no longer what you want now, MAKE a NEW ONE and MOVE ON. That's it and that's all there is always going to be to it!

In time, you will learn to trust yourself and make the decisions faster and better as well as learning to not regret them in the first place anymore - even if they are causing you pain. That's why learning to love yourself no matter what, is key to helping you not get stuck in the beating yourself up cycle.

"What if I don't know how to love myself? I haven't received love in the past. I don't know what that looks like."

The truth is, we DO know what love is! We spend too much time in our heads and our minds convince us that we don't. But I can tell you, when you are in the presence of a person who loves themselves and shows love to you, a shock will travel throughout your body. You won't be able to deny it, for sure.

One time, there was this coach I hired to help me with my English. During our first encounter she made me speak about something I am passionate about and then challenged me on some of the things I said. At the end she said, (I will never forget her words): "You are a very engaged and engaging woman, and for the big heart that you possess, you're not taking up much space!"

I knew she was right, it hit me so hard and made me want to cry.

You do know how to love yourself. It's pretty much like courage in that you've been wired that way. You are pure love. You came out of Love. I'm not talking about the sexual act but about God. You came as pure love in spirit and you probably taught everyone love in the very short time that you were a baby. Some things might have changed afterwards, but for a brief moment, you were nothing but pure love, with trust and faith in your carers. You didn't have doubts. You didn't have your mind telling you what to do. You trusted your body to do its thing. And you survived.

You're here now, reading this and taking charge of your life and becoming this amazing super human being. You can only do this because you love yourself too much not to offer yourself the chance of a life lived with laughter, joy and happiness. YOU ARE LOVE. Start believing that and see your life change.

"What if I can't tell faith from fear?"

When you are in doubt about whether you act in fear or faith - check your body. Your body never lies. You will sense fear as a contraction, a tight feeling in the pit of your stomach, tension in your arms, headaches and you will not be able to feel relaxed in your body. When you're in faith, trust and joy, you feel expansive. Your body feels relaxed, wants to stretch, expand, grow - it's like wanting to hug the whole world. It's open. That's your cue. Don't listen to your mind - listen to your body. The way you did when you were a baby so you could alert your parents when you needed something.

Look, we could spend all day and never finish this conversation. Everything that I say can be met with an objection. At every turn there can be a "BUT". It's up to you now to recognise that and understand that you won't have it all figured out. The only way to do so is to get the process started. With every step you take, you will be given the chance to figure the next one out. And so on and so forth. Circumstances will never change if you come up with all the possible scenarios for it to go wrong. What's wrong is always available but so is what's right, as Tony Robbins said.

Just focus on what's right and keep taking action. You can never fail with this approach.

CHAPTER 7

THE DIRECTION TO TAKE

G reat! As we are getting close to the end of the book you have three options now:

1. Do nothing. Put this book back on the shelf, thinking that maybe tomorrow you will feel like doing something about it. And repeat the same story over and over again.

   OR

2. Start implementing right away. I've made it really easy for you. At the end of the book you will find an excerpt from most of the chapters with the tools and the actions to take, plus blank pages to write out your thoughts/actions. Start where you feel the least resistance. And go from there. There is no "RIGHT" way. There is going to be your way and you will only find it by taking the first step. So go now, to the end of the book and start with the first tool you feel called to use.

Some things won't come easily to you. Others you will need extra support with, which is alright. That is why there is also a THIRD option. One in which you reach out to me so I can help point you in the right direction.

3. There are several ways you can do that. Either through my website: www.laurahurubaru.com
or via
Facebook: https://www.facebook.com/laura.hurubaru/ by sending me a message. I also have a FREE Facebook group where I offer a lot of free coaching for the women who engage actively in it, called Business Women on Fire: Your Signature Business Quest. This is the link to join:
https://www.facebook.com/groups/649922172060910

Don't let dust settle on this. Don't put it off for tomorrow. Reach out and connect with me on these channels today, right now! You'll thank yourself later!

Looking forward to seeing you and learning more about you!

CHAPTER 8

THE JOURNEY TO LOVE

No path is easy. No path is hard. No path is better. No path is clearer.

I remember as a child I used to go to church every Sunday. There is a particular story from the lectures about Jesus that stuck with me throughout my life. The story is told of a man who goes to Jesus, wanting to trade out his cross for a better one. He tells the Lord: "I see the crosses that others are carrying and theirs are much more bearable than mine. Why does my cross have to be so cumbersome and heavy? Other people carry their cross with ease and mine is hindering my day to day life."

Jesus leads the man to a room full of crosses. Some are big and others are small. The man is instructed to put down his cross and then go and select a new cross. The only stipulation was that once he had made his selection he could never complain or exchange his cross again.

He searches for hours on end. The big crosses were just as he assumed, very large and very heavy. He knew there was no way that he could ever carry those crosses. The smaller crosses were shockingly painful. Some had stickers that stuck out and constantly rubbed you on the shoulder or back, reminding you of the timber beams you were bearing. Others were oddly shaped and rubbed the neck raw.

Finally the man came upon a cross that was perfect for him. Not too big, but not too small. There were no sharp prodding objects and it rested perfectly on his shoulder so it would not irritate him as he carried it. The man cried out, "Here it is Lord."

Jesus asked the man, "Are you sure? Remember there are no trades or exchanges and no more complaining about your cross."

The man replied, "I am sure. This is the perfect cross for me."

To which Jesus replied, "My child, that is the cross you carried in with you today."

The truth is that you can cry and moan and bitch about the hand you've been dealt, but in the end you are going to be the only one who can save you. No one else will come to save you. If you understand that and take responsibility for your own life, things will turn around, just because there's no other option but to figure it out. With awareness, discipline and courage, if you take each step in front of you, you will start seeing the light at the end of the tunnel.

Time is the best friend you have and Self Love will carry you when you cannot. With commitment to yourself and to the connection with your higher self, you will find the strength and the power to push through whatever life will throw at you.

And know that you are not alone on your journey. You will have a lot of guidance as well as support, as long as you reach out for help and accept that we all have had giants to support us towards our dreams.

Let GO and let GOD. Trust the process. Take inspired action and have patience with yourself.

Can you see now how, by doing what I have laid out in this book, the sky is the limit?

Can you see how nothing is impossible when you know that you are the creator of your destiny and you've mastered the tools to help you design the life that you want?

Can you see how each of the steps described is interlinked with the other, and really that's why it might take longer to see some results as you are still "learning how to walk"?

How confident would you say that you are right now, on a scale from 1 to 10, that if you take consistent action, even if it's a small action, you will see the changes you are expecting to see?

If you're not pretty confident, what's missing? How can you take everything you've learned in this book and make it work for you so that you feel 100% sure?

If you feel inclined, you can also send me a note to contact@laurahurubaru.com. I might include your suggestion or help with your particular case in a future book.

To your success! I am one message away!

END OF THE BOOK TOOLS AND NOTES

I love reading books, but only the books that I feel have something inside their covers to teach me. An idea to take, a tool to use. As such, I like the practical aspects of books and how they can be used as guides.

This book is not for your leisure. It is for your growth. Have it accompany you until you feel you can skip through life again. I've collected the tools I have presented to you throughout the book, just here and you can utilise the blank pages to allow you to take notes right away. Or you can come back to the tools I shared at a later time. Implement them when they feel right for you, without having to struggle to find them and go through the book again. I hope you will find the book, as well as the tools useful.

If they helped you I would like to learn about it. So don't forget to leave a review on Amazon. Other women might be inspired by it and you would have changed a life in the process.

Chapter 4.

Let me ask you this: *What if everything you think you know about yourself isn't true?*

What if I told you that there is no predefined destination?

What if I told you that there is no 'right way'?

What if I told you the only way is YOUR way?

And that if you allow yourself this, you can invent yourself and change it anytime you want to?

Will you take me up on exploring how this might look like for you?

Great! Pick up a piece of paper and a pen and find a space where you can just be with yourself.

Answer these questions in as much vivid detail as you can, like you would describe a movie on paper:

If you were to let your spirit soar - what would you create?

How would you experience yourself daily?

If you were to be a magical being - what would you be? (You can make up one of your own.)

If you were to possess a magic superpower what would that be?

What magic will you create in your life daily?

Let your imagination flow. You are the author of your book! You just need to become a blank canvas first.

And don't worry about not making sense. Right now just learn to trust the creative side of you. The 'how' will show up when you've made the decision to go for it. I shall expand more on this further on.

Chapter 5.1.

Questions you could ask yourself to help you be effective in your journaling and receive the awareness on why you feel the way you do, or behave the way you do:

1. What's upsetting me about this situation?
2. What pisses me off/angers/saddens me about this situation?
3. What do I think it will happen if...?
4. What's the worst that could happen if that was true?
5. What do I need to learn in order to deal with this effectively?

6. What am I refusing to see about myself in relationship with this situation?
7. What do I need to take responsibility for in creating this situation?
8. What are my next steps?

Chapter 5.2.

To guide you I give you two laws:

- Always assume you're sabotaging yourself.
- Everything you experience is of your creation.

Always assume you're sabotaging yourself - tools to build awareness

- Think back to a time when you were nudged to change your life yet you chose to ignore it and the feeling and the messages kept coming back to you over and over again until something happened. See if you can pinpoint this moment!
- Now think of a time where you heard the voice telling you something and you did it right away; maybe it was to leave a relationship which wasn't serving you? Maybe you quit a

job where you were not fulfilled? In these cases the voice stopped.

- Can you look at this instance and determine if it was the same voice? If it is, then that's the voice you need to become more familiar with.

- Some things to help you along the way; Pay attention to where the voice is coming from. Is it in your head/outside of you, from your left or right, from the front or the back, what tone of voice is that, how loud/soft it is? The more you pay attention to these elements the easier it will become to recognise it.

- And as a final check, when you tune into it and really listen to it, you will start noticing a sense of peace and calmness in your stomach. That's the voice of complete faith and trust. When you follow it you expand. When you go against it you contract.

Everything you experience is of your creation - tools to build awareness

Look at the world around you and treat it as a mirror:
- If you either admire or hate a person remember to think to yourself: I am THAT!
- And whether you like or dislike the situation you're in, ask yourself: what part of me created or aligned itself with this particular situation?

When you think I am THAT, and you completely dislike the person, ask yourself:

- What part of you allowed them to be in your life and what part of you gave them permission to behave the way they do?

- Where you might behave in a similar way?

Chapter 5.3.

Ask yourself this: if you were truly divine light and your purpose is to shine as brightly as possible, how are you honoring the light that is you? How do you show yourself that you love and respect yourself?

How do your actions reflect love?

Tool 1:

Think of a person who you believe loves you unconditionally (if you can't think of one think of God). What will they say to you now about this? How much will they agree with you? And if they were to guide you to more self-love, what would their advice be?

If you're having trouble with this let's do a visualising exercise (read it first and then do it):

Tool 2:

Take three deep breaths and close your eyes. If it helps you can have a nice, soft song playing in the background.

Imagine you're a star in the sky. And now imagine how big you are, what shape you've got, how do you radiate the light, what colours do you radiate, do you also create sounds as well? Just imagine yourself being this star.

Then imagine God has placed you in a certain spot in the sky. You are amongst other stars. Notice how big they are, what their light is like and anything else you want to notice at this moment. Now imagine it's night and people are staring at the sky. They notice a sky full of stars. They can't tell them apart. What do you believe they think about you? About the other stars close to you? About stars generally? About the sky?

Now imagine God comes back to you and gives you advice: what will HE tell you?

Allow for the words to come. Don't stop them. Allow for the vision to continue for as long as it wants. And when you open your eyes, write down the advice you've received.

Chapter 5.4.

Spend time in meditation imagining the situation resolving itself miraculously. Play in your mind movies of all kinds of 'happily ever after' scenarios until you feel no emotions at all. It can take ten minutes, or it can take you half a day. Really allow yourself to go deep and exhaust all possible positive scenarios. Even the most outrageous ones. Especially those.

Ideally, the emotional charge of the situation will go away after a while. And from that place ask yourself: what do I want to do about it?

If you don't receive an answer, let your mind work the problem through in the subconscious and put it to rest for a day or two. And try again. Repeat this process until you find a resolution.

Chapter 5.6.

When you've burnt the boats there is no other option but to take the island!

What promise will you make to yourself first and foremost today? Right now?

What promise will you make to your God/Creator that will help you be happy and free and have what you always dreamed of having?

What's your version of burning the boats to get to the life that you want? Right now?

How can you burn the boats?

Write your answers on post-it notes and have them displayed in multiple places, so that your subconscious gets programmed with them. Put them on your phone's screen saver, on your laptop, in your bedroom and everywhere you are bound to see them.

You can also send me your promise to contact@laurahurubaru.com.
Use the subject line: "My promise to myself is:..."

Chapter 5.7.

Tool 1:

On a scale from one to ten, one being a person who said that they want to lose weight, but with the next chance they get they are in the fridge eating cake, and ten being the person who, even when Covid was going on, bought an exercise bicycle, a trampoline and they exercised indoors daily.

Where would you say you are with your level of commitment in terms of putting in the time?

Where would you say you are with your level of commitment in terms of putting in the energy?

Where would you say you are with your level of commitment in terms of putting in the financial resources to get the help to create these results in your life?

Tool 2:

If you were to die tomorrow, would you still be happy with what your mind is telling you?

Or would you make a new decision? Would you be determined to find a way?

Go back and look at your daily actions. Do they reflect this truth? Or not so much?

What is it you truly want out of this life? If absolutely anything was possible, and you had a magic wand, what does the perfect life for you look like?

Why do you want the things that you want?

What happens if you don't get them? How would that make you feel?

Tool 3:

Imagine you're one year ahead in the future. Your life has dramatically changed since you've done these exercises. And you're writing a letter to your old self, as you are now in the present moment. You are writing a letter in which you thank her for taking the action and making the decision to take responsibility for her life.

Describe how your life looks now (one year into the future) because she decided to make a change and because she put in the work. Tell her all the details. Don't leave anything out. Sign it. And read it every day. You can also record yourself reading it and listen to it daily.

Chapter 5.8.

Tool 1:

Take some time for yourself and start journaling:

- Think of times where you succeeded against all odds; what were they and what three things can you acknowledge yourself for?

- If you asked your best friend about the top three qualities they see in you that they believe are priceless, what are they?

- If you were to be completely honest and loving towards yourself, what are the top three qualities you love about yourself?

- Daily do this, either in the morning, before you start your day or in the evening: ask yourself: what can I acknowledge myself for yesterday/today?

  Don't move on until you find three reasons for which you should acknowledge yourself.

Tool 2:

Here are some ideas to acknowledge and celebrate yourself with every step you take:

- Register for a class or workshop on a topic that interests you, just for fun.
- Enjoy a nice meal alone or with a friend or loved one.
- Listen to music you love and sing or dance like no one is watching.
- Buy yourself some flowers or a plant.
- Draw, take an art class, create a piece of art.
- Brainstorm your own.

Chapter 5.9.

Tool 1:

Think of all the parties involved in the negative situation, including the part of you that created it or the part of you which got hurt and cannot get past the hurt.

Keep repeating the "ho'oponopono prayer" to each party, over and over again until you feel at peace, and there is no tension nor tears which need to be released.

"I am sorry.
Please forgive me.

Thank you.

I love you."

And then change it a little bit and repeat the process again using this prayer:

"I forgive you,

Thank you.

I am sorry.

I love you."

Tool 2:

Think back to a time where you made a terrible mistake that you have not yet completely forgiven yourself for.

Journal everything in relation to the situation, what was it, what happened, what did you do, how you contributed to it and so on. Then ask yourself what you need to forgive yourself for in relation to this situation and then follow the process I've just described.

When you're done and feel at peace or exhausted, write how that made you feel. Look for ways that it helped and search for all the other reasons you need to do this. When you are able to release the stuff from your chest in this way, you will feel like a newborn baby again.

Chapter 5.11.

Find some quiet time and space and imagine you are Love stranded on the island and Time comes in a boat to save you. Write down everything that is happening like you would write a screenplay for a scene in a movie. Let your imagination flow and connect to the characters. Picture it in such a way you can describe it to someone so they can 'see' it too.

Now use the following blank pages to journal out your answers.